PRAISE FOR *DON'T QUIT IN THE DIP*

"More than ever, God needs His Church to press in and move forward into a destiny that is above and beyond... to take back what the enemy has stolen. This doesn't happen when you sit in the dip. You were never created to live there! DON'T QUIT IN THE DIP is the resource that will help you to step out of the 'dips' in your life and move into the fullness of the champion God has called you to be!"

—Christine Caine, activist, international speaker,
and bestselling author of *Undaunted*, *Unexpected*, and more

"Shaun brings a powerful mixture of encouragement, inspiration, and practical tools to help you lower the volume on the nagging voice that is telling you to fold. DON'T QUIT IN THE DIP will help you hold on through hardship and hold out for victory."

—Levi Lusko, pastor, Fresh Life Church,
and bestselling author of *I Declare War* and *Swipe Right*

"If you're determined to reach your highest potential, then quitting should never be an option. In DON'T QUIT IN THE DIP, my friend Shaun Nepstad reminds us all that even in life's lows, we can find the purpose and strength to keep moving forward!"

—John Bevere, minister,
co-founder of Messenger International, and
bestselling author of *Honor's Reward* and many more

"In this amazing work, my friend Shaun Nepstad teaches the necessity of a life skill that is extremely important but often overlooked. The skill I'm referring to is resilience. This book, DON'T QUIT IN THE DIP, is an amazing example of the power of perseverance and a blueprint to do more than endure hard times, but to also overcome them."

—Dr. Dharius Daniels, author of *Relational Intelligence*
and lead pastor of Change Church

"Founded on the truth of God's Word and forged through his own setbacks, this book is more than a spiritual pep talk to keep going—it's an indispensable guide to why and how we persevere as we walk by faith."

—Chris Hodges, senior pastor of
Church of the Highlands and bestselling author of
The Daniel Dilemma and *What's Next?*

DON'T QUIT IN THE dip

STAY FOCUSED ON GOD'S PROMISES FOR YOU

SHAUN NEPSTAD

New York • Nashville

Worthy
Hachette Book Group
1290 Avenue of the Americas, New York, NY 10104
worthypublishing.com
twitter.com/worthypub

Originally published in hardcover and ebook by Worthy in August 2020.
First Trade Edition: August 2023

Worthy is a division of Hachette Book Group, Inc. The Worthy name and logo are trademarks of Hachette Book Group, Inc.

The publisher is not responsible for websites (or their content) that are not owned by the publisher.

Worthy Books may be purchased in bulk for business, educational, or promotional use. For information, please contact your local bookseller or the Hachette Book Group Special Markets Department at special.markets@hbgusa.com.

Print book interior by Bart Dawson

Library of Congress Cataloging-in-Publication Data

Names: Nepstad, Shaun, author.
Title: Don't quit in the dip : stay focused on God's promises for you / Shaun Nepstad.
Description: First edition. | New York : Worthy, 2020. | Summary: "Heal from yesterday's pain and find hope for tomorrow with this inspirational guide for Christians—and learn how God's faithfulness is working for your good, even when times are tough"—Provided by publisher.
Identifiers: LCCN 2020000153 | ISBN 9781546015383 (hardcover) | ISBN 9781546015352 (ebook)
Subjects: LCSH: Christian life. | Spiritual healing—Christianity. | God (Christianity)—Faithfulness.
Classification: LCC BV4501.3 .N465 2020 | DDC 248.4—dc23
LC record available at https://lccn.loc.gov/2020000153

ISBNs: 9781546015376 (trade pbk.), 9781546015352 (ebook)

Printed in the United States of America
LSC-C
Printing 1, 2023

CONTENTS

*I dedicate this book to my wife, Dianna.
Thank you for your unwavering faith
and steadfast resilience, anchoring me
during the times I was tempted to quit.*

FOREWORD

BY JOHN C. MAXWELL

The desire to quit when the pressures of life mount is a strong and tangible force. It's a part of the human condition, and every leader from every arena will face this temptation throughout various seasons of life. But the great news is each time our paths intersect with the desire to quit, we have a choice: A choice to grow. To change. To *not* quit.

As I look across the landscape of our generation, sometimes I wonder if "not quitting" is becoming rarer and rarer. I'm not referring to career or outward success; I can see that in abundance. I'm talking about the discipline of not quitting in our characters, our marriages, our parenting, and in our generosity of love toward one another. We need more voices to speak into these areas of our inner lives and to lead this generation toward success.

Don't Quit in the Dip by my friend Shaun Nepstad is a powerful and much-needed resource for all of us. One thing this book reminds us of is that we have the option to not quit, no matter how impossible our circumstances seem. But Shaun points out something even more crucial for us to understand: you and I were never designed to give up! While the desire to quit might be woven into the fabric of our human condition, so also is the resilience and the fortitude to stay in the fight until we experience victory.

This book inspires and offers very practical strategies to build a lifestyle of not quitting, even in the most challenging times. It also will help you to reach out to others struggling to get out of their dips and valleys. I encourage you to get out your pens, to not be afraid of marking up these pages, and to not stop reading until you finish every page.

—John C. Maxwell, #1 *New York Times* bestselling author
and leadership expert

SECTION ONE

Chapter 1

MOVE, COUNTERMOVE

You. Can't. Quit. There is a story told of a chess champion who is on vacation. Also an art connoisseur, he finds himself wandering through the hallways of a prestigious art gallery. One masterpiece stops him in his tracks and captures his full attention. It's a painting of a chess game. But this is no ordinary chess game. On one side of the board sits the devil, leaning back in his chair with a fiendish grin, confidently tapping his fingers on the table. On the other side sits a young man in utter terror, clenching his teeth, wringing his hands, sweat dripping from his brow. The painting is titled *Checkmate*. It appears that the young man's soul is dependent on the outcome of the game—and he's about to lose.

The chess champion is so taken with this painting that he cannot look away. As his eyes scour the chessboard, his mind begins calculating. When a gallery custodian happens by, the chess champion asks, "Excuse me, sir. You wouldn't happen to have an old chessboard lying around, would you?" The custodian says, "I think I might. Let me check in our break room." He quickly returns and gives the board to the chess champion, who sets it up to match what he sees in the painting. He looks down at the board and back up at the picture repeatedly until every piece is exactly in its place.

After studying the board and the painting for several moments, he steps back and crosses his arms, and a smile creeps across his face. He lifts his voice in the quiet hallways of this seemingly abandoned art gallery and says, "Young man in the painting, I sure wish you could hear me right now, because I've got some good news. The devil only *thinks* he has won, but I've been studying the board, and there is a move he has missed! If you could see what I see, the whole nature of this game would change. Not only would this move save you from defeat, but it would also help you win the entire game!"

This legend, first told in the 1800s and brought to life for me by Tony Evans, is one of my favorites. Maybe it's because I can relate to the young man in the painting, knowing I have given my best attempt at the chess game of life but still have felt cornered. Checkmated. I've had unfulfilled dreams that looked like they would never come true. Slumped back in my chair and ready to give up, I have wished a chess champion would shout out the move that would turn things around.

This slumped-down place in life is what I call "the dip."

THE DIP

When you're in the dip, you can see where you want to be, but no matter how hard you try, it seems you can't get there. You begin to lose hope and doubt you'll ever reach it. The dip is where your dream is just out of reach and you feel stuck. We all have a dream, but there is always a dip before you get there. Sadly, most people give up in the dip. But successful people don't quit in the dip and they're the ones who see their dream fulfilled. We've all been in a dip at one point or another. Maybe you're there now.

None of us have the perfectly filtered life we present on social media, right? Every person, even the ones who seem to have everything together, has at least one area in life that isn't what they want it to be. So we sink back in the chair, staring at our life chessboard, and believe our situation is hopeless and give up.

The dip can be your health. You want to get in shape, attempting every diet fad and workout routine, but nothing is working. The scale ain't moving. When it comes to losing weight and stepping on the scale, there's no such thing as "too naked." You're taking out your contacts from your eyes, exhaling every ounce of air from your lungs, and stretching your arms high to try to defy gravity. Every little bit counts. Or so we think. So discouragement sets in, along with the desire to eat your emotions.

Maybe it's your career. You know there's more in you to express, but there seems to be some invisible ceiling keeping you from reaching your potential or landing that dream job. If only someone would just give you a chance. So you lower your expectations and trade in your hi-def dream for a low-res version of reality.

What about your marriage? You're giving your all, but things are not getting better and you're even contemplating divorce. If marriage is such a sacred relationship, why isn't God swooping in to save the day?

It could be that you're single and looking for a spouse but you just can't find Mr. or Mrs. Right and you're tempted to settle for Mr. or Mrs. *Right Now* instead.

The dip is also where you might stand, wondering, *If God has a wonderful plan for my life, why is He so slow to reveal it? Does He even see me here in this place?* It feels like you have one piece of a ten-thousand-piece puzzle and don't know where to begin.

It's where anxiety and depression have crept in over the years.

You thought you could conquer them alone, but now things are getting worse.

It's trying and trying to get pregnant, but all signs point to it never becoming a reality.

It's where throwing in the towel seems reasonable, and feels like your only option. You feel outsmarted by the enemy. Checkmated.

Do I have your attention?

The young man in that painting is facing the biggest challenge we all face when we are in the dip: the urge to give up. He's stressed, he's filled with doubt, and he simply cannot see how any outcome will be anything other than a clear defeat. He has lost faith and is about to quit in the dip. And just like him, many of us want to give up when we can't see any hope for a positive outcome. But let me encourage you.

When we are ready to quit in the dip, we have a God who is just getting started! God doesn't see as we see! He says, "My thoughts are nothing like your thoughts and my ways are far beyond anything you could imagine. For just as the heavens are higher than the earth, so my ways are higher than your ways and my thoughts higher than your thoughts" (Isaiah 55:8–9 NLT).

When we are ready to quit in the dip, we have a God who is just getting started!

Just as that chess champion saw a winning move that the young man couldn't see, God sees what we don't see in our lives. We see impossible, but He sees possibility. We see financial ruin, but He sees a path to blessing. We see the diagnosis, but He sees the way to healing. God sees the end from the beginning when all we see is our past and our present.

We see a dip, but He sees another opportunity to show up and work through us and show us just how amazing He really is.

Throughout this book, I'm praying we all begin to see from God's perspective—even when we feel like the young man in the painting, backed into a corner, out of moves, with no place to go. The devil thinks he has won, but with God it's not over.

MOVE, COUNTERMOVE

From the beginning of time, we can see many instances when Satan has kicked back in his seat, full of confidence, thinking he has just thwarted God's plans. *Checkmate!* he thinks…until God turns the tables on him with a completely unexpected move. Let me explain.

God created angels. The angel Lucifer rebelled against God, wanting to share in God's glory himself, so he convinced one-third of the angels to join him in his rebellion. Lucifer, or Satan, thought this was a checkmate. But God banned Lucifer *and* his angelic insurgents from the wonder of heaven to roam about in spiritual desolation.

Then God decided to create man. This being was created in His own image and likeness. Satan did not approve. This led to angelic conflict, and a *cosmic chess game* began to unfold. The devil made his move on the cosmic chessboard, and convinced man to rebel against God. Checkmate for mankind. Or was it? As we watch the biblical timeline of mankind unfold, what we see is a back-and-forth battle. Just when it seems Satan has cornered mankind into an impossible situation, God sees higher and responds with one more move! After the fall of man, God made His countermove: He slew an animal to provide a redemptive covering for Adam and Eve so that the possibility for salvation now entered human history. Move, countermove.

So then it was Satan's turn, and he persuaded Cain to kill Abel, trying to eliminate the godly line so that God's prophecy to provide a Savior for mankind (Genesis 3:15) could never come true. But God had a countermove. He allowed Eve to give birth to a son named Seth, and the Bible says that people began to again call on the name of the Lord (Genesis 4:26).

Satan then responded by getting the entire known world to rebel against God through the influence of his demons. All of humanity was so corrupt that God deeply grieved His creation. However, even with 99 percent of humanity in a cavernous dip, God moved and found one man who feared and believed in the One True God: Noah. He instructed him, "I want you to build a boat on dry ground during the day. And print up some gospel pamphlets with a three-word sermon that says, 'IT'S GONNA RAIN!' and pass those out in the evening." God would then judge the world, save this one family. Move, countermove.

Satan made his next move by finding a man named Nimrod, who built two civilizations—Assyria and Babylon. By bringing the two together, he would create a civilization independent of God, centralized around building a religious tower, otherwise known as the religion of man. Otherwise known as humanism. But God moved and confused all their languages so they couldn't communicate freely anymore.

God went even further on the offensive. He came to a city named Ur and found a man named Abram, and changed his name to Abraham, and rolled out His plan to build His own nation, through Abraham, that would obey. That's when Satan responded by getting Abraham's descendants stuck down in Egypt, held captive in slavery to a man named Pharaoh. God responded by going down to a city named Midian and called a man named Moses. He commanded him, "Go and set my people free."

In their escape, Satan trapped Israel between Pharaoh's army and the Red Sea. But of course, God then opened up the Red Sea, and a million and a half of God's people walked across on dry ground.

In fact, the entire Old Testament is move, countermove. Move, countermove. God moved and Satan responded. Then God conquered Satan's move. However, by the end of the Old Testament, from a human perspective, it looked as though we had a tie. There was no clear winner. Just a humongous dip. In fact, between the last page of the Old

Testament and the first page of the New Testament, there were four hundred silent years where there was no Word from God to His people.

When the New Testament begins, it was evidently God's turn to move on the board because it says, "So and so gave birth to so and so, who gave birth to so and so, who gave birth to Joseph, who was married to Mary, to whom was born Jesus Christ."

It's very important for us to see that up until this time of the genealogies listed in the Gospels of Matthew and Luke, God always found a human and used a human. Even when they were in a dip! That's so encouraging. But this time, at the moment of Jesus' birth, God's strategy shifted. He said, "It's time. I'm tired of all this mess. Let me come on down here and handle this punk myself!"

And God entered human history in the person of Jesus Christ.

Satan was not having it. He felt he must rid the universe of the Messiah, once and for all. He thought that his genius plan was working when Jesus was illegally tried and nailed to a cross. It was there that Jesus would hang and there Jesus would die. I'm sure at that moment the devil folded his arms, and with a confident smile thought to himself, *Checkmate!*

But that's when the most surprising move occurred. Early Sunday morning, just a little before sunrise, Mary Magdalene came running to the tomb and found the tomb was *empty*! She discovered an angel sitting on top of the tomb with a sign that read, *#HeAintHere!* Jesus Christ had risen from the dead, and that was the final move!

NOT CHECKMATED

I would have loved to see the look on the devil's face that day as he tried to put all the pieces of the puzzle together. Standing there defeated in bewilderment and frustration. Thinking to himself, *I don't get it. I don't understand. Jesus, You were dead.* To which Jesus responded in His best

Adele voice, "Hello from the other siiiiiide!" No. Actually, He said, "I am the living one. I was dead, and now look, I am alive for ever and ever!" (Revelation 1:18 NLT). Jesus conquered death, hell, and the grave and now offers forgiveness, hope, healing, and eternal life for every person who places faith in Him! That's for *everybody* who surrenders his or her life to Jesus. Even those who are stuck in the dip. Even me. Even you.

For so many of us, this is what has been going on in our lives. It's been move, countermove. Move, countermove. For some of you, the devil has backed you all the way into a corner, threatening "Checkmate." He has harassed you with move after move after move. None of your countermoves have been successful, and you are tempted to quit. I want to encourage you, though, to not believe Satan's "checkmate" lie. Don't sit there and believe it's over! It ain't over till God says it's over. And last time I checked, God's Word still says that "he who began a good work in you will carry it on to completion until the day of Christ Jesus" (Philippians 1:6)! God doesn't see as we see, and He's encouraging us all not to quit in the dip!

Don't sit there and believe it's over! It ain't over till God says it's over.

That's what this book is about. I want you to know that you are not the only one. Every person on this planet is either in a dip, has just come out of a dip, or is about to go into a dip! It's simply part of the human experience. Just like you, I know what it's like to have a dream that seems unachievable, and I know what it's like to feel stuck to the point where you start believing you will never reach that dream. But I didn't quit. And through it all, God has given me some powerful truths, which I will share to help you reach a place of victory.

Keep reading. Get your highlighter out and keep it out, because in these next chapters I want to help you identify your dip. You'll learn that the dip does not have to be your final destination. There are lessons we can learn in the dip, which can teach us how to climb out of the dip to see our dreams become reality. I know things might not look good now, but hold on! There's still another move left on the board that will not only deliver you from defeat but will also give you the ultimate victory.

No matter how many moves and countermoves you have experienced, God has the final move. And if you will journey with me through these pages, you will learn that not only is God for you, but also He has gone before you and ordered your steps *through* the dip to a wide-open space of victory. So no matter where you find yourself right now, and regardless of how deep the dip seems to be, look back at the board. There's a move you haven't seen yet, but God sees it. And He wants you to win. So...DON'T QUIT IN THE DIP!

Chapter 2

TIME'S UP?

When I was in seventh grade, basketball was my sport. As the point guard, I brought the ball down the court. In one particular game, we were down by two points against our archrivals. You know how bloodthirsty middle school basketball can get. As my teammate inbounded the ball to me, my heart beat out of my chest with the insurmountable pressure. *Don't mess this up, Shaun,* I said to myself. *You got this.*

As I started dribbling the ball down the court, getting ready to call out the next play to our team, the crowd screamed, "Three!"

Wait, I thought. *There are only three seconds left?!*

"Two!" they shouted.

I've got to take this shot for the win, but I'm so far away.

"One!"

I gathered my inner Michael Jordan and launched a full-court shot from the opponent's free-throw line. The ball arced up to its peak and then began its descent. The crowd gasped. There was potential to this shot! Remember, this was for the game-winning points. The ball came down, hit the backboard with a thud, and bounced to the other team.

I heard laughter coming from the stands, and I couldn't figure out why. That was an incredibly hard shot! Especially for a scrawny twelve-year-old. But as they mocked even more, they pointed at the scoreboard and time clock. To my humiliation, there were three and a half minutes still on the clock! They had tricked me! I felt like the biggest moron. The opposing fans had duped me into believing there was no more time left on the clock, and it got me to make a bad decision. I'm still in therapy to this day.

The devil loves lying to you and trying to make you believe there is no more time on the clock. To get you frazzled. To get you to make a rash decision. To get you to believe that it's over. But it's not over yet. Don't quit in the dip, and don't get distracted. There is still more time on the clock. If there is breath in your body, God is not finished with you yet. Yes, there are more mountaintops and challenges ahead of you, but most of all, there is more inside of you. There is still time on the clock, and you and I must not give up. We need to keep playing until the buzzer goes off.

"What's the buzzer?" you ask. I'm glad you brought that up. God's buzzer is found in 1 Thessalonians: "The Lord himself will come down from heaven with a commanding shout, with the voice of the archangel and with the trumpet call of God" (4:16 NLT). So until we hear that buzzer, it's still game on! In other words, we keep going until Jesus returns.

I've heard it said, "We are not fighting for victory; we are fighting from a place of victory." This concept inspires me and reminds me that the book of Romans tells us that through our union with Christ, He has made us more than conquerors. Jesus has already defeated the entirety of Satan's kingdom; all we have to do is walk out that victory in our lives, through Him. Having said that, many of God's finest men and women throughout the ages have known what it feels like to be so tired of it all. You and I aren't the only ones who have felt pressed against the clock, wanting to quit in the dip. But like those who have gone before us, we need to put our faith in Jesus. Each time that we do, He will show up and build our faith to believe Him for more. If you are living in a dip right now, then you are in really good company. I know exactly what that feels like.

> Jesus has already defeated the entirety of Satan's kingdom; all we have to do is walk out that victory in our lives, through Him.

WHEN THE DIP KEEPS GETTING DEEPER

My wife, Dianna, and I started our church when I was twenty-four years old. You have to be half-crazy to start a church at twenty-four. Well, our city was in luck because I'm three-quarters crazy, on my daddy's side. I'm actually a fifth-generation pastor on both sides of my family. It's like the Mafia. And to prove my crazy, at the same time, Dianna and I had four girls under the age of two. You read that right. A two-year-old. A one-year-old. And newborn twins! Obviously the Nepstads are great planners. Ha! Have you ever seen a double stroller? We had three in a triple stroller and one on a leash. Don't judge. You do what you have to do to get by as a young parent. I was a diaper-changing machine, changing sixteen diapers a day!

We began the church with twenty-two people, and on launch weekend we had a hundred and five. God gave us a dream to reach thousands of people, and I thought in six months there wouldn't be a building big enough to house us. Well, that didn't happen. Reality was, we definitely had some challenges and started to feel stuck in the dip.

When we launched, the only place we could find was a cafetorium. That means we had an elementary school cafeteria with a stage. When we rolled in to set up every Sunday, it smelled like tater tots, gym socks, and that nasty box of lost-and-found clothes. Welcome to church, people!

We didn't have enough adult-sized chairs, so I headed to our local hardware store and found those white picnic chairs that you can stack up to a thousand. They had a three-dollar option and a one-dollar option. Which one do you think I went with? Yeah, I took the chair for a buck. Why would I pay two dollars more for the same chair? I bought a hundred of them. In our cafetorium, we set up the white plastic chairs in the center section and then positioned rows on the sides of our other hard, metal chairs. Our church had options.

This fiscally brilliant choice of the one-dollar chairs was working out great…until a solidly built man visited one Sunday and decided to sit in the middle section. Now, sitting in one of these white chairs was not an issue. The problem occurred when he decided to get comfortable and lean back while I was preaching. Now, these chairs are not built for that. They're built for four on the floor. Those two back legs were straining to hold his weight and they finally gave up the ghost—right in the middle of my sermon. The chair collapsed, and so did he. *Crash!* His arms went flailing as gravity won yet again. They don't teach you how to respond to this type of situation in Bible college. Not wanting to embarrass him by drawing attention, but also not wanting to ignore him, I paused and asked, "Are you okay, brother? You…you good?" I was mortified. He never came back. I know what you are thinking: *You should have gone with the three-dollar chairs!* You're in good company. Dianna thought the same thing.

The dip got worse. Three months into the church, we got kicked out of the school because they needed a month to redo the flooring. We frantically searched for another school, but after we'd settled into school number two, the city made a new law. Any church renting inside a school could only be in that school for one year, and then they had to move. That's Cali for you. So now we're playing musical churches!

We'd meet here for one year, then move. Meet over there for a while, then move. Just when we'd hit momentum, it would be time to relocate. That's not a strategy you're going to find in a book on church growth. It was like our dip kept getting deeper.

Our prayers were finally answered when we were able to graduate from the elementary school cafetoriums to a high school theater. We were so excited! But this only proved to be worse. Yes, we had a theater, but we were not allowed any classroom space near it. The kids' classes were on the other side of this enormous campus, so by the time parents checked their children in to the classes and walked back, church would be half over. To make matters even worse, for some reason the facility's heater was always on—even in the middle of summer! I don't think you heard me correctly. I didn't say the air conditioner was broken. I said the heater was on, pumping hot air…in the summertime…in California. It was like hot breath on the back of your neck. When it was 100 degrees outside, it felt like 189 degrees inside. God bless our greeters. They would still try to serve with a good attitude. Sweating profusely. Putting deodorant on their foreheads. Greeting people at the front door with a weary half-smile.

And you should've seen the people coming into church. They'd walk in and walk right back out. One lady said, "I love Jesus, but this feels like hell." As a church planter, all I could do was scream, "Nooooo! Don't go! We'll give you a bottle of water."

The dip was turning into a chasm. On top of our location debacles, I went into the hospital because of severe stomach pains. I don't mean just a regular stomachache. Since the age of thirteen, I had dealt with unbearable stomach pain that would come out of nowhere. By this time, the episodes had become more frequent and more intense, to the point where I would be doubled over on the floor for six hours, writhing in pain. Nothing gave relief. One day our drummer had to physically pick me up and carry me to the car and race me to the emergency room. It got so bad that I was in and out of the hospital and losing blood.

Finally, they kept me for three weeks. I was not allowed to eat or drink anything, not even ice chips. Test after test. They put me on some medication that made me hallucinate. I dropped down to 125 pounds, and I was losing my mind. Again, this type of situation was not addressed in Bible school.

People were asking, "What's happening?"

And I would answer, "I don't know."

"What should we do at the church?"

"I don't know."

"Who's speaking this Sunday?"

"I don't know!"

I didn't know anything. The church, my family, all of us were scared, and it felt like the dip had morphed into a bottomless pit. I felt like time on the clock was ticking frantically to the buzzer, and the stress of not having done what I felt God wanted us to do was overwhelming me.

The doctor diagnosed me as having ulcerative colitis. It's brought on by stress and worry. The pain was excruciating. I spoke with a mother who also suffered from this condition, and she said it was worse than childbirth. So I did what any loving husband would do: I threw that in my wife's face. I told her, "Don't you talk to me about pain. You don't even know…"

On a serious note, I felt I was losing my mind, the church, the dream, my sanity. Every day, I'd cry out to God. Just when I was about to quit in that dip, God healed me, and I haven't had a pain in sixteen years! He was right there with me the entire time, teaching me, strengthening me, and walking me through it. In fact, while I was in that hospital room, God took me deeper with Him and spoke some things to my heart, and I wouldn't trade that season for anything. Maybe the dip you're in concerns your physical health. I'm praying over you that Jesus will bring healing to your mind and your body. God is the great physician, and He hasn't closed up shop.

After weeks, I was able to return to work, but our church was not completely out of the dip. Another frustration arose when our congregation grew to three hundred pretty fast but then just stopped growing. Plateaued. Stuck. No growth for seven long years. That's 364 Sundays; 364 sermons; 364 load-ins and load-outs. We were trying everything. I thought all you had to do to grow a church was preach really hard and have good music. That might work for some people, but that was not working for us. Three hundred is a great number, but we had a dream to reach so many more people. And by the way, the wrong question to ask is, "Isn't the church big enough?" The right question is "Who's still missing?" Every number represents a soul. God is passionate to leave the ninety-nine to go after the one who is lost. We wanted to build a church around the final words of Jesus, to reach the world. The reason we struggled with the three hundred was because of the stagnancy. Seven years is a long time to feel like there is no growth. We were stuck in the dip.

Have you ever sludged through a season of stagnancy? Maybe in your business or your career? Or dealing with a volatile ex-spouse and a blended family. Or a child who seems to always choose to go the wrong way. Or maybe it's an addiction you struggle with every single day. Whatever the dip, you feel like there's so much more you want to see, but you're not seeing it. And it's killing you. That's exactly how I felt. It doesn't matter the issues surrounding the dip. Stuck is stuck.

We had a dream to reach thousands of people, and we truly believed it was a God-breathed dream. We had so much in our heart to accomplish, but none of that was coming to pass. I was growing impatient. Tired. Frustrated. Angry. So much so that, in my heart, I actually threw in the towel and started begging God to show me another pastor to whom I could hand over the church. Someone who could take it where it needed to go. Just as my middle-school basketball game went, I could hear the echoes of "Three!...Two!...One!" screaming in my mind. Only this time it wasn't the opposing team shouting it—it was me. I was beginning to truly believe the lie that it was over.

Thank God it's not over until *He* says it's over!

IT AIN'T OVER

The frustration is real when a dream is growing inside your heart, but the reality of that dream seems to tease you just out of arm's reach. In that space, my tendency is to march ahead and make whatever needs to happen happen. At any cost. And as you just read, for the first season of our church, that cost was my health. In addition, the more I tried to fix it on my own, the deeper the dip grew.

I knew I couldn't go on like this. I needed to do something different in how I was leading the church or give up altogether. In the next chapter, I'll tell you what I eventually did, and how I held on in that dip for seven long years. There is still a lot more of our story to share with you, but first I want to tell you what I learned in the dip.

When I look back, I realize I went through a few stages of the dip. Proverbs says, "There is a path before each person that seems right, but it ends in death" (14:12 NLT). I was the poster child for this proverb because I *thought* I was doing everything right, that I would get out of the dip by trying harder. But each progression only caused me to sink lower until my heart and mind were filled with doubt.

First, I thought that everything would just get better over time. When you're frustrated and discouraged because you're not seeing movement or change, people will often say, "Just give it time." But I have learned that time doesn't automatically fix things. If we aren't doing the right things, time often

Time doesn't automatically fix things. If we aren't doing the right things, time often makes things worse!

makes things worse! The longer you're in a dip, the more you begin to lose hope, to give up, to grow numb, and to become angry and cynical. Inaction and simply waiting aimlessly for "time" to step in and hand you a "Get Outta Dip Free" card is not going to do anything. Once I figured this out, I swung the pendulum waaaay over to the other side.

From that stage, I moved into believing that I just needed to work harder. Yeah, that's it. Just give it the good old-fashioned blood, sweat, and tears effort. But that went over like a pregnant pole vaulter. Yes, hard work is important, but it's deeper than that. When we are striving and doing everything in our *own* strength, our bodies cannot handle the physical and mental stress. We weren't designed to carry this load by ourselves and outside the dependence on Christ, who strengthens us. It'll end up taking such a toll on us physically, mentally, emotionally, and spiritually. Finally, doubt settled in my heart and mind like a heavy fog on a San Francisco night. I couldn't see the vision set before me, and that doubt began to choke out any enthusiasm to keep going. My heart bailed. Do you know what that feels like? It's profound, because your heart can bail long before your body does. My heart bailed even though I kept showing up at work. I was going through the motions, but I was a shell of who I was when I'd started. Hollow on the inside. I'd hear stories of how great things were going for other people in ministry and I'd just get mad. It's not that I didn't want them to succeed. I just didn't understand why that wasn't happening for me.

I fell deeper into the dangerous game of comparison in the dip. That's as bad as beating up the guy who just lost in the boxing match. I would see where other people were and then I'd look in the mirror at where I was and want to smash the mirror. I hated where I was, that I wasn't where I thought I should be. Envy and jealousy don't help in the dip. It's like the devil hands you these two shovels of envy and jealousy, and without even knowing you're doing it, you go right ahead and dig your own dip deeper and deeper.

Be careful you don't let feelings lead you over principles. Feelings are up and down. Don't make decisions based on how you feel, make decisions with a future focus. Because when you're in the dip, you won't feel like you should keep going. You'll want to quit because you believe there's no more time. Don't listen to that lie. God still has more time on the clock. Don't listen to the devil yelling out, "Three! Two! One!" That's just a trick to get you to make a bad decision.

Refocus. Regroup. Re-up your dependence on God. He's the head coach. Pay attention to what He says, and run the play. Then run the next one. And the one after that. It's never too late to start doing what's right. The most exciting plays in a game are buzzer beaters. Last-second turnarounds. Comebacks. I know you think it's over. But it's not over. There's still time left on the clock. Get back up and play ball. You can still win this thing. Trust me, I wish someone would've encouraged me with these words while I was in one of my deepest dips. Read on.

Chapter 3

UNDER THE DESK

Tears were streaming down my face as my body was folded up under my desk like origami. I had just preached my heart out that Sunday, and I was exhausted and overwhelmed. Earlier that week, I had been teaching boldly, and now I was hiding from the world, hoping no one would find me like this. I felt at the end of my rope, and that desperation had me crying out to God, barely able to squeak out the words: "I can't do this anymore! Find someone else. I'm done!"

Under that desk, I felt pressed into a corner. No way out. No hope. I was in a huge dip with what felt like a stagnant church, countless failed strategies, a long battle with my health, and detour after detour with our church location. I wanted so badly to quit. But I just kept seeing the faces of the precious people in our congregation. Deep down, I knew there was still purpose for my life; I just wasn't seeing it. At this particular moment, all I could see was the underside of my desk.

Have you been there? Are you there now? If you are, you're not alone. I know things don't look good now, but every person who has done anything great has had a season in a dip. But the dip is not your final destination. You may not be able to see a way out right now, and neither did I.

What do you do when you don't know what to do? What do you do when the dream inside of you is not matching the reality that's in front of you? It's going to sound cliché and elementary, but oftentimes we overcomplicate things. We're willing to try the newest strategy, follow the latest teaching, hop on the trendiest spiritual bandwagon, but we roll our eyes at the basics. So, what did I do when my dream didn't match the reality in front of me? We started a prayer meeting. I catch on fast. I was seven years in before I finally said, "Hey, guys, maybe we should pray."

What do you do when the dream inside of you is not matching the reality that's in front of you?

A simple, unsophisticated prayer meeting was our plan, where a few people got together to pray. I wish I could say it was amazing. It didn't feel amazing at all. It felt awkward and a bit too late. At our first meeting we had eight people total, and six were my family. They had to be there. We would gather once a week, with me sometimes jumping on the keyboard, and we'd fumble through prayer. I banked on Scriptures like Jeremiah 33:3, where God said, "Call to me, and I will answer you; I will show you wonderful and marvelous things" (GNT). I told God, "I'm not seeing 'wonderful and marvelous.' I'm seeing *mediocre* at best. But I will take You at Your Word."

By the way, so many people feel awkward praying. Most people, when asked to pray publicly, would rather die. They say, "I'm not good at praying." What does that even mean? Can you talk? Great! That's all prayer is: talking with God. Why are we so intimidated by prayer? I'll tell you why. It's performance anxiety. We get scared because either we are trying to impress people when we pray, or we attempt to sound like someone else when we pray. God is not impressed when we are trying to impress. But He is impressed with honesty and transparency and faith. Prayer is simply talking to God. If you are doing that, whether privately or publicly, you can never go wrong.

In our prayer meetings, we would show worth to God. We'd spend time telling Him how much we love Him. We'd thank Him for what He's already done. This part is huge. Thanking Him first changes your heart and how you approach Him. Remind yourself of everything He's already given you. Grace. Mercy. Love. In our prayers, we'd tell Him what we needed help with. We'd make sure we were in line with what He wanted in the Bible, and then we'd thank Him in advance for coming through for us. I told God, "I can't do this on my own! I need you. And I confess my dependence completely on you."

Let me encourage you: set aside time—put a reminder on your calendar to talk with God every day. Do it when you're at your freshest. Otherwise you'll fall asleep or get a little spiritual ADD like me. I start praying, and about two minutes in, my mind wanders and I start thinking, *Did I have pizza twice yesterday?* Get a good prayer journal or outline to help you.

When you're in the dip, praying will remind you that God is in control. He can walk with you through the dip. He can guide you and carry you through people talking about you at school. He can guide you in your marriage and give you wisdom and strength, even when there's been an affair. Where else are you going to turn when your child has walked away from you or God? What will help you hold on when you feel God has called you to a specific place, but it's taking too long? What defense do you use when everyone around you is telling you it's time to give up?

Prayer! Don't hold it in. Don't try to do it on your own. Talk with God. He said He would answer and show you wonderful and marvelous things. Take Him at His Word.

I made prayer my top priority and number-one strategy. Why not, right? Nothing else I was doing on my own was working to pull us out of the dip. And through those times of prayer, God got my attention. He reminded me that when I didn't know what to do, I needed to go back to the last thing He said to do. For me, this was it: *Build this church.* And when I wanted to quit, I needed to remember that God directed us to start this and He would be faithful to finish it. I was searching for a way out, so why wouldn't I go to the One who knows the way? Who is the way? Jesus told His followers, "I am the way and the truth and the life" (John 14:6). I kept seeing those three hundred faces in our church. God had given me a supernatural burden for them, and I knew I couldn't bail out on *them.* Even though I wanted to, I couldn't. And God changed everything!

If God did this for me, He can do it for you. We all go through seasons in life that we never expected, that sneak up like a sucker punch to the gut, or that feel like a slow crawl through the Mojave Desert. When you find yourself there, don't get discouraged. Don't fall to your knees in defeat. Instead, bend your knees in prayer. Get out from under the desk and pray, because there's power in the posture of prayer.

CLIMBING OUT OF THE DIP THROUGH PRAYER

In that prayer meeting every week, God began to open my eyes to not only see strategy about how to build people but also to recognize some key relationships to help us on our journey. Anytime I have grown in my life, it has been because of great people stretching me.

About a year into the prayer meeting, applying key systems to help people discover their purpose and a place for them to make a difference, our church began to grow. At the start of these prayer meetings, we had been stuck at three hundred people. Again, it wasn't about the actual numbers, because three hundred is a great number. We just felt God had put a dream in our hearts to reach so many more. After seven years of zero growth, during year eight and after implementing all the wisdom God had provided through those prayer meetings and helping people discover their God-given purpose to make a difference, the church grew to five hundred. Well, that's almost double. The next year, eight hundred. Then sixteen hundred. Two thousand. Three thousand. Five thousand. If every number represents a soul, then every number is important. Every life is valuable and we're trying to make the biggest difference in our lifetime.

We still have more in our heart to do. But here's a big question: Where would all these people be if we had quit in the dip? We have seen thousands place their faith in Jesus. We have witnessed so many marriages restored, with more children born into their families afterward. There are human beings who wouldn't even exist if we had quit in the dip. You can always find reasons to quit in the dip. Because quitting in the dip always seems reasonable. But prayer helps you focus on what's beyond the dip: "Let us not become weary in doing good, for at the proper time we will reap a harvest if we do not give up" (Galatians 6:9). Don't quit in the dip!

> You can always find reasons to quit in the dip...But prayer helps you focus on what's beyond the dip.

In winter, you want to take the longest and hottest showers you can. Running to the shower, early in the morning, you crank the water on as hot as it'll go but you never jump in right away. That would be crazy. The water is never hot immediately. It's ice-cold because of all the water that has been sitting in cold pipes all night long.

You've never turned the water on and reached to feel the temperature with your hand and then in utter disappointment turned it off. No! You know that if you let the water run long enough, hot water will come. It's just a matter of time for the desired result to show up. No matter how cold those pipes are, you know hot water is on its way. Why do we so often have more faith in our hot water heater than we do in God? Don't turn off your faith. Don't relinquish your trust just because you're not seeing what you want right away. It may not come immediately but at just the right time, God will send the answer. Just don't shut Him off. God's answer is hot water through cold pipes.

DENIED

The church was finally growing! We went from one service on a weekend to two. From two to three. Then three to four. Then to nine! It all happened so fast, I was surprised that we were actually out of the dip. Or were we? Yes, the growth was phenomenal, but I realized there were a few more dips in front of us.

Remember, we were still portable. Which means we were setting up and tearing down every week in schools and a community center. We did this for—are you ready for it?—thirteen years! Sometimes when we coach church planters who complain and say, "We've been setting up and tearing down for, like, fourteen months," I say, "Fourteen months? Try thirteen years!" That's the time spent from kindergarten to graduating the twelfth grade! Our team was so well-versed in setting up and tearing down, they could do it in their sleep. And I was ever on the lookout for *any* other possibility than a portable.

There was a building in our city that a friend and I would frequently talk about. "If that ever becomes available, that space would make a great church." It was a hardware store, open warehouse style, forty-three-thousand square feet. Guess what? Eventually, it *did* become available, and we swooped in to make an offer. The next nine months was a roller coaster of ups and downs.

First, the owner asked for a crazy amount of money, to which we lowballed. The proverbial paper was shoved back and forth across the table until we met in the middle and our church put $50,000 in title. We had a verbal agreement…until he broke that agreement and signed a contract with someone else! I was livid. But then that offer fell through and he came back to us. He said, "Let's go back to our original agreement." I said, "That was messed up. But okay." We really wanted this building, so we started negotiations again, but when he asked for the $50,000 in cash instead of placing it in escrow, we said no way! I wasn't born yesterday. Turns out, since he couldn't make his payments, he had to hand the keys over to the bank.

We shifted our conversations to the bank, who said since they hadn't seen a church grow as fast as ours had over the last few years, they were sure we'd have no problem getting the building. There was only one hoop we needed to jump through first. That building was in a shopping center, and the neighboring office supply chain had the approval rights for the entire center, so we had to request an approval letter from them.

We did some reconnaissance and contacted a bigwig in the corporation, and he assured us closing the deal would be no problem. He told us they do this all the time. I said, "Look at God!" All that was required was a written letter of request from us and they would approve it. So we sent one in. But when we got the letter of response from them, it was a big, fat NO. "What do you mean no?!" I said back to the paper in my hands. "I thought we were good to go!" The letter's excuse said, "You're not a benefit to our store." I immediately replied, "Well, I'll be a benefit. I'll buy all my highlighters from you." I began thinking of anything we could do to show them we would be a benefit.

We wrote back and promised them we would encourage our folks to shop there. We knew they were the lowest-producing store in the region at that time. And we thought this store would be shut down, just like all the other stores in the region. We offered them $150,000 to help them, just as a sign of good faith. Perhaps we should've used a bit more tact because they did not respond kindly. The letter read: "Please be advised that *our* position remains firm and this shall serve as final notice of our **denial** of such request."

I read their letter and thought, *Really? You didn't have to bold and underline the word denial.* That was harsh. I felt like someone had punched me in the stomach. We had been working on this deal for *nine months*. There are no other buildings near our portable church that could work. I felt like I heard a voice say in my heart, "It is now physically impossible." It was a done deal.

I remember that day so vividly, me in our bedroom reading that gut-wrenching news. All the work. All the time. For nothing. I was beyond frustrated. Can you imagine all the emotions? I was so angry that I hit my bed (because it was soft). When Dianna walked in, I read it to her and said, "Can you believe this? Nine months of negotiations and it's over?"

Dianna turned to me and said with complete confidence, "That's okay. God's got this. It'll be all right."

I wanted to say to my wife, "Well, thank you, Miss Holy Spirit. Miss Woman of Faith. But *my* faith is still in process here." But I'm glad I kept my mouth shut, because right then, the statement I had heard in my broken heart resounded: "It is now physically impossible." Only this time I felt God respond, "Yeah, it *is* physically impossible. And that's exactly when I start getting to work." Of course it was physically impossible, with no physical solution. What we needed now was a heavenly intervention.

When this office supply chain had firmly shut that door in my face, it looked like a good and reasonable time to quit. But so much had transpired from that day when I was origamied under my desk, so close to giving up. God had come through in countless ways for us that even though we felt we were sliding into another pit, we knew we couldn't allow ourselves to keep sinking. We had to trust God. Period! Even when we could not see with our natural eyes the work of His hands.

Chapter 4

GOD IS AT WORK

I went to a play once. I'm not proud of that. But my wife is a classically trained opera singer, so I decided to take her to see an opera. It was called *Phantom of the Opera*. She informed my novice mind that this was not an opera. It was a musical. I said, "Then they should take it out of the title because that's confusing."

Anyway, we sat through this musical for about an hour; then the curtains closed. "Huh," I said. "That's a weird place to end." As I was getting up to leave, Dianna replied, "Babe, it's not over. This is intermission." I was glad she wanted to get out of our seats and walk into the lobby to get snacks and soda. After about twenty minutes, there was a bell that sounded in the lobby, and I think I was the only one who didn't know this was the universal signal for the audience to head back to their seats. When we walked back into the theater, the curtain was still closed. Nothing had changed.

At least I *thought* nothing had changed, because when the curtain opened on the second act, I was stunned that *everything* had changed.

While we were in the lobby stuffing our faces with snack food and soda, there was an entirely different crew, working behind the scenes. In a matter of twenty minutes, when the curtain opened, there was a completely new set. New costumes. New props. A totally new configuration. Even if we had stayed in our seats, we would not have seen anything happening. The transformation was going on out of sight, behind the scenes.

In the same way, just because we don't see God moving does not mean He is not working. He is working behind the scenes of our lives. In fact, He is *always* working all things together for the good of those who love God and are called according to His purpose (Romans 8:28), even though many times when we are in the dip, we can't see it. We need to let Him work.

Despite the debacle of trying to buy that building, we knew we had to trust that God was working behind the curtain. We dug deeper in prayer and felt it was time to do something crazy. I already told you I'm three-quarters crazy, so you shouldn't be surprised by what happened next. On the very next Sunday, I told the church all that had transpired. I showed them the letter, with the bolded and underlined **denial**, and then proceeded to roll out my plan. With a shaky voice I said, "We're all going to write letters to the CEO of that company to ask them to reconsider their position. Don't be mean or nasty, but as concerned citizens of this community, let's ask them to reconsider."

> Just because we don't see God moving does not mean He is not working. He is working behind the scenes of our lives.

Everyone in the church had the same facial expression you have right now. I could see the wheels turning in their heads like, *Our pastor is an idiot, but try not to let your face show it.* I asked ushers to pass out envelopes to the people raising their hands, showing they wanted to participate. Looking around the congregation, I pointed out hands to the ushers to help during this awkward moment. "Sir, would you like one?"

I asked, only to realize, "Oh, you were just scratching your nose? That's okay. Ushers, give him one. And give that lady two; she's pregnant." I was desperately using humor, trying to help people to join me in this absurd plan, which I wasn't even sure was from God. Sometimes when we get an idea in the atmosphere of faith-filled prayer, we have to walk it out. Standing in front of the congregation that Sunday, I was starting to doubt, but I had to try.

We wrote letters that week, but we received no response from them. The next Sunday I stood up and said it again: "Hey, guys, let's keep writing those letters." Another week went by with no response. I was certain this would be the week we would hear an answer. I was wrong.

It was the third Sunday of me facing the congregation, beginning to see how pathetic my plan was and saying meekly, "Hey, everyone. I know we haven't heard anything, but if you haven't written a letter, could you please write one this week?"

Driving home that day, I felt like it was over. I couldn't imagine getting up there one more week to ask them to write letters. My mind began reeling. Are they even doing it? Are they actually writing the letters, or are they just saying they are? How could I know for sure? Did I completely miss God? Maybe this whole thing was a dumb idea, a pathetic attempt to somehow manufacture the response I wanted to hear. Maybe I was just delaying the inevitable? Yep. Probably. Next week, I would just have to eat crow, thank the church for trying, and move on. At least for the next couple days I'd be out of town, so I wouldn't have to face anyone until Sunday.

TUESDAY IN THE DIP

It was Tuesday at 4:37 p.m., just two days later. I had just landed at the Birmingham, Alabama, airport, and I was standing at the baggage claim waiting for my bag. Funny. Life sometimes feels as if you're standing at a baggage claim, waiting for an answer to come around on the conveyor belt. Everyone else was getting their bags. Everyone else was getting their answers. And yet where was my answer? When was mine going to come around the corner? Well, as I stood at that baggage carousel, I got both my bag *and* my answer. A text message chimed on my phone, and I looked down to read three little words that would change everything.

Did you hear?

I called the guy who had been working this deal with us for the building. On the other end of the line he yelled, "THEY CHANGED THEIR MIND!"

What? What does this mean? All of a sudden, my luggage became irrelevant. "What do you mean they *changed* their mind? How? Why? Who said?" I was bewildered and shocked.

Their letter read, "Our office has been flooded with letters. It has not fallen on deaf ears. We have reconsidered our position." AND...they did not even take our $150,000!

Are you kidding me? I could not wait to tell the church. That next Sunday, I got up onstage and did what any good pastor would do: I milked it. They didn't have a clue. Somberly and with a straight face I said, "I know I have been asking you to write letters the past three Sundays. I know we haven't heard anything. I know it's frustrating." I showed the denial letter on the screen again. I was really building it up. "But I want to let you know I received another letter from them, and it says..." I hung my head to hide my smile. After a cruel, pregnant pause, I screamed out, "THEY CHANGED THEIR MIND! WE GOT THE BUILDING!"

Our church went crazy, with a greater level of excitement than you've seen at any sporting championship event. In utter amazement, they jumped to their feet as if their team just scored the winning touchdown at the Super Bowl. People were jumping and cheering while others began to cry. We had waited so long in the dip. But God—even though nothing seemed to be advancing in the natural—was working behind the scenes. He was working behind the scenes and He made a way where there really wasn't a way. It was the fulfillment of a dream we had waited on—and doubted—and almost gave up on for so long in the dip.

NOT ABOUT A BUILDING

So many times, we were tempted to quit in the dip. But God wasn't finished yet. This old hardware store used to be a place where people could get tools to fix their homes; now it would be a place where people could get tools to fix their lives, through Jesus Christ.

Now, having said all of this, it's not about a building. What God did in the midst of this building was one big sermon illustration for what He wants to do in your life. It doesn't matter how bad it looks. It doesn't matter how hopeless it feels. It doesn't matter how deep the dip is or how long you've been in it; God is bigger than your dip.

On that Sunday, a lady came up to me and said, "When you asked us to write a letter, I thought it was a dumb idea. I only wrote one because you asked us to, but I didn't believe it would change anything." I thought, *Well, thanks for the vote of confidence.* But she continued: "Now that I've seen God move here, this is giving me faith to believe God for my family." See what I mean? It was never just about getting a building; it was about God building the HOUSE, meaning the people who make up our church, and teaching us to trust Him in the dip!

So, in what area in your life has the devil backed you into a corner and gotten you to believe you've lost? That you'll never succeed? That you can't win because time is up? Is it your marriage? Your kids? A dream? Where in your life is there a pile of facts that say it can't happen?

Be encouraged today by remembering that God is bigger than the facts. The facts say one thing, but God's not limited to the facts. He sees the facts, steps over the facts, and says:

"Your marriage can be healed!"

"Your children can come back to God."

"You're not destined to a life of emptiness and brokenness."

"Your body can be healed."

Jesus said, "In this world you will have trouble. But take heart! I have overcome the world" (John 16:33). He wants to bring you hope and healing! Don't quit! I know things don't look good in the dip—they never do!—but that's because our vision and understanding are obstructed by the dip. It's just like when Dianna and I were at *Phantom of the Opera* and the set changeover was obstructed by the curtain; while it looked to me like nothing was happening, dozens of crew members were busily taking care of every detail. Just because you don't see God moving does not mean He's not working. He's working behind the scenes. We need to trust that even in the dip, God is taking care of every detail. Let's look past the dip and gaze at our all-powerful and all-knowing God who makes this promise to us: "And we know that in all things God works for the good of those who love him, who have been called according to his purpose" (Romans 8:28).

> God works for the good of those who love him.

JOSEPH'S DIP

A guy in the Bible named Joseph had a dip. A thirteen-year dip. He had dreamed that his brothers would bow down to him. They hated him before he blabbed his dream, and now they hated him even more.

After the brothers threw Joseph into a pit and began contemplating how to kill him, one of the brothers showed mercy. He suggested they just resort to human trafficking, and they sold him as a slave to a band of travelers on their way to Egypt.

I'm sure Joseph couldn't believe his own family tossed him into the pit. It must've hurt so much for him to overhear their plans to sell him.

Joseph was now a slave in the house of a powerful guy named Potiphar. God gave him favor until Joseph was elevated in status and in charge of everything. Things were going great until Potiphar's wife threw herself at Joseph, and when he rejected her advances, she lied and accused him of rape. Once again, Joseph was thrown into a pit. Only this time it was a pit of prison. Years went by. Eventually, he met a couple of Pharaoh's servants—a cup-bearer and a baker—and helped them understand their dreams that had been haunting them. When the cup-bearer got released, Joseph in return simply asked that the guy put in a good word for him with Pharaoh. The guy forgot for two more years. Thirteen years total since his brothers betrayed him. Thirteen long years in the dip. Hell on earth. He had every reason to quit in the dip, but he didn't.

As you read Joseph's account in Genesis, every once in a while, tucked into the pages of this Old Testament story, you'll read a phrase that is repeated: "And the Lord was with Joseph." Try reading that again in a British accent. It makes it sound better. God was with him even in the dip. He was working behind the scenes, even when it looked like nothing was happening. Even when Joseph's situation seemed to have gone from bad to worse, the Lord was with him.

The Pharaoh had a series of dreams he couldn't figure out; in fact, none of his officials could interpret the dreams. He was desperate and asked if *anyone* could tell him what these nightmares meant. This finally sparked the cup-bearer's memory of the friend he met while in prison, and he said, "Oh yeah! There was this guy with me in the pen. Joseph. He could do it." So they fetched Joseph and cleaned him up. They presented him before Pharaoh, and sure enough, God gave Joseph the interpretation of the dreams. There would be seven years of plentiful harvest followed by seven years of famine. But that's not all that happened... Pharaoh then elevated Joseph to be second in command of the entire nation of Egypt. This was not just rags to riches, this was dip to destiny. Good thing Joseph didn't quit in the dip.

Just as Joseph predicted, there was a terrible famine in the land. But since God had given Joseph knowledge of this upcoming tragedy, Joseph commanded the nation to save silos full of grain from the previous seven years of plenty. Now Egypt had so much food that it became the wealthiest nation in the world. People were coming from all over to buy food from Egypt.

One day Joseph was sitting there officiating all the rations, and guess who showed up? His brothers. To buy food. They all came and bowed down to him, just like in his dream so many years ago. But they didn't recognize him because he was wearing his Egyptian garb and thick Mac eyeliner makeup. Can you imagine the emotion that must have flooded through Joseph? All the anger. The frustration. The betrayal. And though he had the power and the means to get revenge, he stopped and gave them vision. A new perspective. You've heard of 20/20 vision. Let me give you 50/20 vision:

Genesis 50:20 says: "You intended to harm me, but God intended it for good to accomplish what is now being done, the saving of many lives."

Joseph got it! He was in a dip. A deep, horrible, life-altering dip, but now with a different perspective he was able to see what I hope you see through this book: YOUR DESTINY IS ON THE OTHER SIDE OF YOUR DIP!

Too many people quit too early. Thank God that Joseph didn't. Where would all the thousands of people have been had Joseph quit in the dip? God used the dip to work some things out in Joseph's heart and character so that He could elevate him to rescue a nation. On top of that, he saved his entire family, who went on to become the twelve tribes of Israel.

You can't quit in the dip. Just like for Joseph, there are people waiting for *you* on the other side of your dip. You might feel like me, under my desk, crying out to God to rescue you or to pick someone else to complete your calling. You might feel like Joseph, betrayed by those he loved and thrown into a dip for several years. But God sees you. He wants you to trust that even though you can't see it just yet, He is working behind the scenes. Even those things that have been done to you, things that intended to harm you, God can use them to sharpen, strengthen, and propel you. He can turn it around for good, allowing the circumstances of that dip to launch you into your destiny. Don't quit. Other people are counting on you.

SECTION TWO

Chapter 5

THE MUSIC TRUCK

Our daughters never knew what the ice-cream truck was. I feel partly responsible for that because when it came around, I told them, "Girls! The *music* truck is here!" Remember, Dianna and I had four girls in under two years. When you have that many kids, at a young age, while you are still trying to navigate being a new parent, you're just trying to survive. Ain't nobody got time (or money) to deal with the ice-cream truck as it drives through your neighborhood every day.

For about two years, our daughters thought the sole purpose of this "music truck" was to drive around and spread cheer through our neighborhood by playing music for little kids to come outside and dance. Every time they heard the music truck, they would run to the door. I would even open the door because I knew they wouldn't chase after the truck. They would just smile, wave, dance, and shout, "Hi, music truck. Hi!"

Needless to say, we had a lot of confused drivers wondering, *Do you want me to stop? Do you want ice cream?* They would slow down, but

I'd wave them on, communicating to them, "Keep on driving, buddy." When the girls finished dancing, they would wave and say, "Bye, music truck. See you tomorrow!" Now, you might think that was cruel, but do you know how much money I saved in those two years? Four dollars for an overpriced ice-cream sandwich? And multiply that by four girls. I don't think so! For two whole years, my plan worked brilliantly, and I gloried in my wit.

Until I was outwitted by another. My plan came crashing down in one fell swoop the day I drove to pick up my girls from Grandma's house. Dianna's mother. My mother because of the law. With a couple of them still in their diapers, my girls dashed out to meet me with sparkles in their eyes that were not there when I dropped them off. Gasping for air, they tried to find the right words to communicate the exciting news they wanted to share. Our eldest, who was three and the only one able to communicate intellectually, said, "Dad! Guess what?" I asked, "What is it?" She took a deep breath and yelled, "THE MUSIC TRUCK HAS ICE CREAM TOO!"

And in that moment Grandma ruined everything. From then on, every time they heard the music truck, they were not content with just dancing. They wanted hard, cold cash to buy overpriced ice-cream treats. Their mind-set was changed forever, and they would never again be tricked into believing only music came from that truck. Oh no. Now they knew there was more. SO much more than just dancing to sweet-sounding jingles. There was a host of different ice creams to choose from, and they weren't happy until they had ice cream all over their faces. Thank you, Grandma.

WE ALL WANT TO KNOW IF THERE IS MORE

We all have a feeling deep down in our soul that there has to be more. Somewhere there is a woman wondering if her dreams will ever come to pass. There's a businessperson who has achieved many successes and yet still feels empty. An employee who is going through the motions every day, and even though nothing is necessarily bad, nothing is necessarily great, either. Deep down in all of us is a gnawing feeling that there has to be more than what we're currently experiencing. There has to be more meaning to life. More fulfillment in life than just dancing for a music truck. Certainly hidden within the music truck of life there is a freezer filled with a host of dreams and experiences that will surprise our souls.

Deep down in all of us is a gnawing feeling that there has to be more than what we're currently experiencing.

So what's keeping us from experiencing the life God has for us? One problem is we all have three thousand messages screaming at us every day. Voices on social media, polished to perfection. Voices of comparison. Voices on TV, on the internet, from friends, in the music we listen to. All these voices are telling us we don't have enough. Their messages are so loud and frequent that they stick with us and we begin to believe them and allow ourselves to be steered in the wrong direction. My friend Rob Hayes-St. Clair told me: "The voice you make the loudest in your life is the voice that will determine your future."

The question *Is there more?* is coupled with a strong desire to fulfill that longing. What we need to realize is true fulfillment doesn't come from more of something. "Somethings" like more stuff, more activity, more applause, more ice cream from a truck might satisfy us for a moment, but being satisfied for a moment is a far cry from experiencing fulfillment.

There *is* more! A lot of things in our world promise "more," but there's actually only One who can deliver more, and that's Jesus. Only He can offer us the deep satisfaction that our hearts are longing for. He promises us, "A thief is only there to steal and kill and destroy. I came so they can have real and eternal life, *more* and better life than they ever dreamed of" (John 10:10 MSG, emphasis mine). The devil came to steal, kill, and destroy. Jesus came to bless, give life, and restore.

We have an innate desire for more; discontent is the human condition. Either you haven't accomplished all that's in your heart, or you *have* achieved all your earthly goals only to discover it doesn't satisfy. What you thought would deliver the ultimate fulfillment has failed to deliver, and you still feel empty.

There's something inside of you and me that believes there's more than what we are currently experiencing. God put that feeling in your soul. His thumbprint. It's His purpose bubbling up in us to draw us to Him, to find everything we long for *in Him*. It's called the abundant life. He's providing heaven as our ultimate and great reward, but He also wants you to live this abundant life on earth. For those who put Jesus first, they "will be repaid many times over in this life, *and* will have eternal life in the world to come" (Luke 18:30 NLT, emphasis mine). It's not either/or; it's both/and.

Many of us, like my daughters with the music truck, don't know there is more until we taste a little of God's goodness. But the devil doesn't want to just keep you from experiencing more; he wants to kill, steal, and destroy all that you've had, have, or dream of. Jesus came to give life. It is real life. It is eternal life. It is *more* than you can think or imagine, and it can begin today.

I was walking down the street one day and saw a girl wearing a shirt that said "More, More, More!" and I began to think, that is what we all want. Advertising companies know this, and they play on that. They all promise more.

"Fifty percent more, free!"

"More TV channels."

"More horsepower."

We all want more! Usually, when we envision more, we think of *that* certain car, or *that* particular house, or *that* dream job with *that* dream salary, or *that* perfect relationship we've created in our minds. So what keeps you awake at night as you think, *If only I had ________, then I would finally be content*? But again, the problem is nothing in this world can permanently satisfy. Fulfillment does not come from more stuff; it comes from more of God. It comes from a relationship with Him and then walking in His purposes for your life. That's it! But most people quit in the dip before they discover this.

> Nothing in this world can permanently satisfy. Fulfillment does not come from more stuff; it comes from more of God.

I believe every one of us is asking three questions, either directly or indirectly:

What's my purpose?

Does my life matter?

Will I ever do anything significant?

Not knowing the answer to these questions can lead you into a dip. And you can't climb out of the dip just by getting more stuff. Stuff is not the answer. King Solomon was the epitome of this. He was the most powerful man in the world, and he had it all. All the fame. All the money. He lived a life of luxury on steroids. He had anything and everything that his heart desired. The houses. The latest chariot with twenty-two-inch rims. The women. Who needs a thousand concubines? He thought he did. And not only did he have everything, but also the Queen of Sheba came to visit and was blown away by his wisdom and riches. People would've loved to have been him. Here was a guy who literally had everything, and yet he still wasn't satisfied.

He was a great example of someone who needed more. The first part of his life, he was the greatest king Israel had ever known. He built the temple, he was known throughout the land as the wisest man alive, and he established an enormous kingdom. But his desire for more didn't end well. It wasn't that he didn't have enough—it was that what he had wasn't right. At the end of his life he wrote a book, which starts off pretty depressingly:

> "Meaningless! Meaningless!" says the Teacher. "Utterly meaningless! Everything is meaningless." What do people gain from all their labors at which they toil under the sun? All streams flow into the sea, yet the sea is never full. To the place the streams come from, there they return again. All things are wearisome, more than one can say. (Ecclesiastes 1:2–3; 7–8)

Okay. Not the best way to open your first chapter. You don't want to depress your readers in the first sentence. But that's how he felt. He couldn't take it anymore and basically screamed, "Life is meaningless!" He had it all but had nothing at all. There's a difference between "meaningless more" and "meaningful more." It's not quantity; it's quality.

Can you relate? Are you searching for meaning in meaningless stuff? Does life feel disappointing and hopeless, and you feel so tired of it all? I think all of us hit a patch like this at some point. Seeking fulfillment in the wrong place can make you want to quit in the dip, and it can put you in the dip in the first place. Remember: *Fulfillment does not come from more stuff; it comes from God.*

What I mean by this is that a real relationship with Jesus is where you find unconditional love, indescribable peace, joy, forgiveness, hope, healing, and so much more. Yes, there's more to life than what you're currently experiencing, but could it be, like Solomon, that you've been looking in the wrong places? It's so frustrating when you're looking for ice cream and realize it's the garbage truck. Solomon finally admitted in the last chapter of his book that purpose comes by putting God first and obeying Him. Or maybe you've been living unaware, as our daughters had, that *more* is even possible? Don't settle for music-truck theology. I'm here to tell you the music truck sells ice cream too.

Chapter 6

JESUS SEES YOU IN THE DIP

There was a fisherman by the name of Simon Peter. He went by both names. He was fishing all night but not catching anything. The next morning, Jesus saw him and called out to him. While sometimes we might not see clearly when we are in a dip, Jesus' eyesight is never blurry. Jesus sees you, even in the dip, and He calls you to more and brings greatness out of you. And that's what He did for Peter.

Luke 5:1–2 says, "One day as Jesus was standing by the Lake of Gennesaret, the people were crowding around him and listening to the word of God. He saw at the water's edge two boats, left there by the fishermen, who were washing their nets." Jesus was teaching a crowd, but these fishermen were not a part of it. After toiling all night, they were still working hard. While everybody else was hanging on Jesus' every word, these fishermen were on the edge, "washing their nets."

Now, the Bible doesn't just use filler. Details are recorded for a reason. Why would the Bible record they were washing their nets? Because they had fished all night, caught nothing, and now they are done. You wouldn't wash your nets unless you were done.

ALL WASHED UP

Jesus saw them wrapping up their night of work and still came over to ask if He could get into their boat and finish teaching the crowd from it. They agreed, but can you picture the look that must have been on Peter's face? He was exhausted, his blistered hands were washing his nets, and then this guy walked over and asked them to go back out. It's like if you've ever worked at a restaurant and you close and lock up at 9:00 p.m. so you can clean up and go home. And then someone comes at 9:05 p.m. asking if you're still open. Jesus got in the boat before Peter climbed back in. He was still washing his nets, wanting nothing but to leave and clock out from his shift. But Jesus is always ready before we are. You need to know that He's just waiting for us to get into position.

In a house with five women, I'm usually the first to be ready, and then I sit there waiting. Waiting. Waiting for them to get ready. Jesus and I have a lot in common. Ha! Jesus said, "I'm going to get in your boat and preach a sermon." And Peter thought, *How long is the sermon?* He didn't want to be there. He didn't want to listen to some stranger. He wanted to go home. He'd had it. He felt like *he* was all washed up.

But for some reason Peter agreed, and for his effort he got a front-row seat to hear the greatest teacher the world has ever known. Peter was in awe. Watch this: Peter was no longer on the edge. Jesus sees you on the edge. He sees you on the edge of disappointment and discouragement. He sees you right where you are. He sees you in the dip. Some of you have gotten comfortable on the edge. You're not too far away. But you're not too close either. You're on the fringe. And Jesus says, "I don't want you there. I want you by Me."

So Jesus taught the crowd from the boat, but His greatest lesson of the day came next. "When he had finished speaking, he said to Simon, 'Put out into deep water, and let down the nets for a catch.' Simon answered, 'Master, we've worked hard all night and haven't caught anything. But because you say so, I will let down the nets'" (Luke 5:4–5).

"Because You say so." That's a powerful clue about how to get out of the dip. In spite of the frustration, Simon Peter obeyed Jesus even though he was saying, "We have worked hard all night and we haven't caught anything. Zero. Zilch. Nada."

As Joseph Stowell once said, this is not fly fishing, where you gently cast out your line and easily reel it back in a second later. This type of fishing involves heavy, wet, soggy nets with weights on them that have to be thrown out and then muscled back in, over and over and over. If you were in the boat, you would have just pulled an all-nighter and would have been exhausted, hungry, and cranky since coffee hadn't been invented yet. These men had tried very hard to fill their own nets, but they had nothing to show for it.

JESUS SEES YOUR EMPTINESS

It's one thing if you're on vacation and you don't catch anything. That's no big deal. I've been fishing and not caught anything before, and I just stopped at the grocery store on the way home and picked up some fish. I told my wife, Dianna, "We caught all this!" and pointed to the spoils that had been wrapped by the grocery store and still had the price tag on them.

However, if this were your livelihood, a night of empty nets would be horrible! They had worked all night and had nothing to show for it. So Jesus saw their nets and asked them, "How's fishing?"

"It's lousy!"

"Hey," Jesus said, "I've got an idea. Let's go out into the deep and get ready for a catch."

They said, "Look, mister, we're professional fishermen. We do this for a living. We know these waters. If there were any fish to be caught, believe me, we would've caught them."

Meanwhile Jesus was probably thinking, *Yeah, but you didn't have Me in your boat.* You need to know that in your own strength, you're not going to catch anything, but when you get Jesus in your boat, all that changes. Proximity to Jesus can alter your perception and provision. When you enter into a trust relationship with Jesus, where He's directing your life, He brings not only calm but also a plan. A plan to get out of the dip.

When you get Jesus in your boat, all that changes. Proximity to Jesus can alter your perception and provision.

Maybe you feel like you've worked really hard in life to fill your nets by yourself. You've tried to fill your nets with relationships. A job. Education. Pleasures. And you keep throwing the net out expecting it to return full, but every time it comes back empty. This is where we have to be brutally honest with ourselves. Ask yourself if this is a true statement: "Everywhere I cast my net, the result is always the same. Empty."

And now you're frustrated. Tired. Empty. Just like Peter, you feel all washed up. Maybe you've even said, "I'm done!" Or maybe your first instinct when a friend has told you about Jesus or invited you to church was, "Look, I'm a professional. If there were purpose out there, I would've found it by now. If there were more to be found, I would've found it."

Many times we can blame our emptiness on the spot. The location. That's what fishermen say all the time: "This spot is no good." So they move to another spot thinking they'll have better luck there. That's why many people move to a different city, take another job, end old relationships and begin new ones, change churches, or whatever. But too often it's not about the *what* or *where*—it's about the *who*. You can change all this and still be empty. Remember, fulfillment doesn't come from more of something; it comes from more of Someone: Jesus.

It's interesting that Jesus took Peter back to the same spot at which they had toiled all night and blessed them with the biggest catch they'd ever seen. You see, all of this is about obedience to the One who blesses the spot. Put yourself in the right place of obedience and God will open up the right door of opportunity.

Jesus sees you on the edge. He sees your labor and your emptiness. If you want more, start doing what Jesus says. Remember, Peter was washing his nets. He was done. He was complaining, stating the facts that they had fished all night and hadn't caught anything. We do the same thing. We list the facts of everything we've tried, as if to say, "If there were more out there in life, I would've found it by now." Peter adds, "But because You said so…" See, there's the difference. There's blessing, protection, and provision because God's Word guides us to more.

Peter obeyed, and the fishermen reluctantly rowed back out, to the same spot they had combed through for hours already. But this time, after throwing in the nets, their eyes got big. They looked at each other in disbelief. They started pulling in the nets, and the nets were starting to snap. I can see them laughing because they had never seen anything like this before. "Hey!" they yelled to their partners in the other boats. "Come help us! There's more fish than we can even pull in!" See, your obedience to God's Word will bless others around you as God blesses you, and then out of the overflow of that blessing, you can bless others.

Remember John 10:10. It's the abundant life that Jesus came to bring both for eternity and here on earth. He loves you. God is a good Father. Remember His nature, and remember His Word, which will direct you and equip you for more: "All Scripture is God-breathed and is useful for teaching, rebuking, correcting and training in righteousness, so that the servant of God may be thoroughly equipped for every good work" (2 Timothy 3:16–17). How have so many gotten out of the dip? By listening to God's Word. The same way Peter did. "Because you say so…" It was never about fish. Jesus just wanted Peter to know the source of all good things. And Jesus wants to lead you to the more you've been looking for.

JESUS SEES THE REAL NEED

Immediately after catching the fish, Peter knew. This was no ordinary man. Peter saw the analogy Jesus carefully and meticulously laid out before him: Peter had been empty and was searching for more. He had been longing for purpose in the monotony of life. His net not only represented his livelihood, but it also represented his life. And when he had allowed Jesus to get into his boat and had surrendered his nets to the instruction of Jesus, the result of his obedience brought about a blessing beyond belief.

Peter fell to his knees at the feet of Jesus and said, "I'm not worthy to be in your presence. I'm a sinful man!"

"Then Jesus said to him, 'Don't be afraid; from now on you will fish for people.' So they pulled their boats up on shore, left everything and followed him" (Luke 5:10–11).

Jesus saw Peter fully; his sin was not hidden from His sight, but Jesus did not come to condemn. He came to give abundant life. He called Peter to stand up, and He prophesied vision into his brokenness. "From now on, you will be so much more than a man who catches fish. You will become a leader who catches people and changes their eternal destinies."

I love those three words of hope: "From now on." Jesus spoke them to Peter, and He is speaking them to you and to me. Jesus sees our strivings and our emptiness and wants to convey the same message He conveyed to Peter.

"Don't be afraid. From now on…"

"I know you've been chasing one empty thing after another, but from now on…"

"You may have been wounded, you may be angry, you may be bitter or struggling with who you are in life, but from now on…"

From now on, life can be different. From now on, Jesus is calling you to more. You can walk in purpose and fulfillment and the abundant life Jesus came to offer. It's not about what you *have been*, but what you *will be*.

So compelled were the fishermen that when they rowed the boats to shore, they dropped their nets. For good. They left everything and followed Jesus. Crazy!

The very thing that Peter had worked so diligently to fill *was* filled—even beyond capacity—and his response was to turn and immediately leave it. While this may have seemed rash to most people, Peter knew that the only one who could deliver more was standing right in front of him. He was willing to give up everything for that "more." So that morning, after Peter had caught more fish than he'd ever caught in a single outing, he walked away from it all. It would have been easier to walk away from empty nets. That would have been no sacrifice. But Peter walked away from full nets. It doesn't say in the Bible that the nets were sold to make a profit. Or what happened to the fish. Peter just left.

Sometimes God allows you to have what you think will fulfill you, only to let you see it's not what you really need. My daughter Alexandra puts it this way: "Sometimes we come to God for what we want and leave with what we need." We need Jesus, not more fish. We need Jesus, not more stuff. Sure, it's nice to have stuff, but stuff doesn't satisfy, no matter how much more you acquire. Abundant life is not about getting more stuff; it's about

Sometimes God allows you to have what you think will fulfill you, only to let you see it's not what you really need.

getting more of Jesus. And with Jesus come love, joy, peace, purpose, meaning, and fulfillment. God sees you in your attempt to find meaning and fulfillment, and He wants you to know today that He is your source. Everything we need is found in Him alone.

In one moment, Jesus changed the entire trajectory of Peter's struggling life. In one moment, Jesus saw Peter in the dip and then lifted him out. Jesus called him to higher heights. Called him to the needs of the people. And Peter would go on to become one of the greatest leaders of the early church.

God sees you. Right here. Right now. He's calling you to more. Peter went on to change the world and help birth the greatest movement the world has ever known. But think for a second: Where would Peter have ended up if all he had done was say, "Thanks for the fish," and go back to life as usual? Thank God he didn't do that. In that split second, he gave Jesus everything.

What about you? Would you take a second to tell God that you're ready to give your life to Him? Completely. To place your trust in Him to forgive you, to cleanse you, and to give you a fresh start. I'll give you the words to pray, but make them your own.

> *Lord, thank you for loving me right where I am. I ask you to forgive me from all my sin. Cleanse me as I place my faith in You. Be my Lord and Savior. From this day forward I will follow You. In Jesus' name, amen.*

Chapter 7

A SECOND DIP

In one episode of the television show *Seinfeld*, George Costanza is at someone's house for a reception following a wake, where he heads over to a table full of snacks. Grabbing a potato chip, he dips the chip into the bowl of dip. After taking a bite, he then double dips the same chip. It's a hilarious sketch because there is another guy, Timmy, standing nearby who witnesses George's infraction and confronts him, saying, "What are you doing? Did you just double-dip that chip?" George is shocked there is even an issue with his double-dipping, which leads to a huge and very hilarious argument.

Sometimes we're shocked at the double dips in our lives. We are totally caught off guard because we don't think that we could be in a dip, get out of the dip, and then fall back into it. Well, sorry for the tough love, but I gotta be honest: you can.

Have you ever come out of the dip and then blown it again? Felt like a failure? And I don't mean just that you messed up a little; I'm talking about a scenario where you had everything going for you and then something happened that caused you to topple all the way back down to the bottom of the dip. Then you became so discouraged with it all. You couldn't understand how you went from being so strong to then getting distracted as your heart started to turn in the wrong direction. If you can relate to the double dip, you're in really good company, because Peter—the guy we talked about in the last chapter—did just that. He was one of Jesus' best interns. One of the twelve closest to Jesus. Yes, even Peter double-dipped.

Here's some context: Jesus' fame was blowing up, and Peter got to see it all up close. It must've been an amazing season. And then it all went south. There were some religious men who had been plotting to kill Jesus for some time, and now they were ready to act. The night before, Jesus knew this was going to happen, that it had to happen so He could die on a cross and pay for the sins of mankind. He gathered all the disciples, His interns, together for what is known as the Last Supper. While the disciples were completely oblivious to what was about to take place, Jesus had a conversation with Simon Peter:

If you can relate to the double dip, you're in really good company...Yes, even Peter double-dipped.

> "Simon, Simon, Satan has asked to sift all of you as wheat. But I have prayed for you, Simon, that your faith may not fail. And when you have turned back, strengthen your brothers."
>
> Peter said, "Lord, I am ready to go with you to prison and to death."
>
> [Jesus answered,] "I tell you, Peter, before the rooster crows today, you will deny three times that you know me." (Luke 22:31–34)

Peter sounded so confident. So sure of himself. He'd come out of the dip three years earlier, and he felt like nothing could sway him now. You know the feeling. Another dip isn't even on your radar. When you're in such a good place, it seems like nothing can stop you.

Jesus dropped a huge bomb, informing Peter that before the rooster crowed in the morning, three times he would deny that he even knew Jesus. Now, this sounded absurd to Peter. He thought there was no way something like that could happen!

After the meal, they all followed Jesus to the garden to pray. Judas, one of the other disciples, betrayed Jesus by leading a small mob into the garden to hand Jesus over to them. Confusion spread among all the disciples, as they were likely thinking, *What's happening? Is this a joke? Why is Judas doing this? He's one of us. After all we've been through, he is betraying Jesus?* The disciples were freaking out. Completely distraught. Scared that the guards would take them too—especially after Peter had grabbed his sword and lopped off one of the servant's ears. So they all ran away. The guards arrested Jesus, and Peter followed the group at a distance. He couldn't believe what was happening. This was not in the plan. This was not on the schedule. It had come out of nowhere.

Word spread fast, and while Peter tried hiding his identity, other people began to recognize him and ask him if he was one of Jesus' followers. He declared, "No!" A second time he was asked if he was a follower of Jesus, and he told them even more aggressively, "No!" In Mark 14:54, we read that people were gathered around a charcoal fire and Peter stepped close to warm his hands. In Matthew 26:69, Peter didn't even have the courage to tell a young girl in the shadows of the night that he knew Jesus. As soon as he had denied Jesus for the third time, the rooster crowed in the background, and the words of Jesus, still fresh in his mind, came racing back to him.

Overwhelmed with failure, Peter was sure he'd lost everything. He'd lost his hope of a future. The plan. He'd lost the relationship with his best friend, Jesus. And as much as he tried to get a foothold, he found the dirt crumbling beneath his feet as he fell back into the dip for a second time.

Jesus willingly went to the cross to die a horrific death while the disciples, save John, hid in fear that they might be killed for their close association with Him. With death lurking all around them, the disciples had been convinced it was over. Checkmate. Even in John 21, after Jesus had risen from the dead and appeared to the disciples before He disappeared again, the disciples were still reeling. Sure, they were thrilled and amazed with Jesus' appearing/disappearing act, but they were absolutely perplexed. *Is the mission back on or not? Are we going to be led by Jesus again, or was His disappearance His final good-bye? What does it all mean?!* Peter had finally gotten so fed up with it all that he said, "I have to do something other than just sit here. I'm going fishing." The other guys said, "We'll go with you" (see John 21:3).

Wait. Hold up. What does the Bible mean when it says these men went fishing? Was Peter like, "Hey, guys, we need a break, so let's go fishing. It's been a crazy three years, and we could really use a day off"? Not even close. They believed it was over. They gave up on following Jesus. Gave up on the dream. They decided to throw in the towel—or, actually, throw in their nets to catch fish again. They were not just taking a day off; they were starting up the old business again! They were quitting and going back to what they felt they could control and be good at on their own. Ultimately, though, Peter had fallen into a dip again.

But don't look at them like they were crazy. We all would've been discouraged too. Imagine following Jesus for three years thinking He was going to overthrow the Roman empire and establish a new kingdom, with you as a major player at His round table, and then He goes up on a cross and dies. Wouldn't you have come to the conclusion that it was over? "We had a good run. Now I have to do something. At least I know I can catch fish." All of us have those moments when we are tempted to go back to what we feel we can control.

They thought they could go back to fishing and be good at it, as they once had years ago on that sea. But they fished all night again and caught *nothing*.

Jesus appeared on the beach, but they didn't know it was Him. He called from the shore, "How's it going? You catch anything?"

And they hollered back, "Nope. It's horrible. There were no fish out there last night."

And Jesus said, "Hey! Here's an idea—why don't you try throwing your nets on the other side of the boat?"

Seriously? they probably thought. *No thank you!*

Then one of them said, "Hey, guys, what's one more cast?" So they threw their nets in the water, and they caught so many fish that their nets began to break.

John exclaimed, "It's the Lord!"

They couldn't believe it. They all looked at each other in amazement. And Peter jumped in the water and started swimming to Jesus. Some would say this was impulsive. I think it was because Peter had sensed his life was about to change for good this time, and he didn't want to hang out in that dip for one more second.

THE POWER OF GOD'S LOVE

When they all got to shore, they found Jesus cooking fish on a fire. In complete awe, they settled into breakfast with their Savior, Jesus. As they were licking their plates clean, Jesus turned His attention to Peter and asked him a peculiar question: "Do you love me more than these?" And Peter, who was always so quick to answer, replied, "Yes, Lord. You know I love you."

Jesus didn't take his word for it. He answered, "I'll know that you love me when you feed my lambs." That sounds weird. Then, a second time: "Do you love me?" And Peter said, "Yes, Lord, you know that I love you." Once again Jesus didn't take his word for it, telling him, "I'll know that you love me when you take care of my sheep."

Can you put yourself in Peter's flip-flops for a moment? First of all, they were not alone. This was not a private conversation; it was on the beach in front of all the other guys. Can you sense how uncomfortable this must have been? Then Jesus asked him a third time: "Do you love me?" Peter responded again, grieved and trying to convince Jesus so they could move on and talk about something else. "Lord, you know all things. You know that I love you." And, you guessed it. Jesus didn't take his word for it a third time and said, "Feed my sheep."

What in the world was going on with this strange conversation? Jesus wasn't telling him to feed literal sheep. All through the Bible, people are referred to as sheep. Jesus was telling Peter to get involved in people's lives and to love them. He was basically saying, "If you love me, then get involved with what I love."

When my daughters were young, I loved Disney princesses. I knew everything about them. Not because I simply loved Disney princesses, but because I had four daughters who loved Disney princesses. What's important to them is important to me. And nothing is more important to God than His children.

A lawyer once asked Jesus, "Which is the greatest commandment?" Jesus answered, "Love the Lord your God with all your heart and with all your soul and with all your mind." The guy only asked for one, but Jesus knew you couldn't divorce the first from the second, so He threw in the second one for free: "Love your neighbor as yourself. All the Law… hangs on these two commandments" (Matthew 22:36–40). Everything God asks of us is birthed out of loving God and loving people.

SHOW ME

Why did Jesus ask Peter, "Do you love me?" three times? Because He was setting the stage for something. If we connect the dots, we see that this is the second time Jesus purposefully performed the same net-breaking miracle to remind Peter of the moment of his calling. Do you remember in the last chapter how Jesus first called Peter? Jesus wanted to take him back to when he first started following Jesus, and with the same miracle He called him back, out of the double-dipped dip, to follow Him again.

If you really study the text, you'll find something else very interesting. On the beach, Jesus was cooking fish for breakfast over a fire. You've heard of the Last Supper? I once heard Joseph Stowell call it the Last Breakfast. It wasn't just your normal fire, though. If you look at the Greek language here, in which the New Testament is written, this fire was actually a charcoal fire. Why that detail? Well, there's only one other place in the entire Bible where there was a charcoal fire—the fire where Peter denied Christ. Why would Jesus do this? Think about it: Isn't it crazy how certain smells can take you back? You smell someone's perfume that reminds you of your mom. You smell a certain food, which takes you back to your childhood eating fresh-baked cookies at your grandma's counter.

Can you imagine what the smell of a charcoal fire triggered for Peter? It probably reminded him of when he denied Jesus. When Peter thought he was alone in the shadows of his failure, Jesus was letting him know, "I was still with you. I saw you, and I still want you." Jesus was re-creating a moment Peter would never forget, one that would have probably haunted him forever. Jesus now turned it into an illustration of reconciliation.

In addition to the fire, Jesus had just re-created the moment of Peter's calling, when he and his fishing buddies had caught so many fish just before they left their nets behind to follow Jesus. With a heart of complete restoration, Jesus did both of these significant acts to let Peter know, "I know you've failed me, but I still love you. I still have a calling for you. I'm still your provider. I'm still your source. I can still use you." Jesus called him out of the dip and back to a life of following Him. A life fulfilling God's purpose.

Is Peter's story also your story? Do you know what it's like to experience a double dip? To fall the second time? Or maybe the third time? Or the hundredth time? Like Peter, I'm sure you have felt like quitting. Like bailing on Jesus. Abandoning the call of God or the dream inside your heart because of a failure. But your failure does not have to be your final destination. Your failure doesn't have to be your finale. It doesn't have to be your checkmate.

> Your failure does not have to be your final destination.

Ask Jesus to forgive you for whatever failure is haunting you, and turn back to follow Him. Jesus could've easily written Peter off, but instead He went to great lengths to convince Peter of his value. Jesus is calling you now. Maybe for the first time, or maybe He's calling you back again. Allow Jesus to take you back and remind you He was there when you failed. Not for shame. Shame isn't from God. But He wants you to deal with the failure. To confess it in the dip so you can be completely restored and reminded of your calling.

For many of us, our starting point with Jesus was that sweet moment when He entered our lives and transformed us. When we were so overwhelmed with His love that we promised to follow Him for the rest of our lives. But for many of us, something happened, and we found ourselves distant from Him. Jesus used Peter as an example to let you know no matter how far you've fallen in the dip, He can reach down and grab you out with His love and grace. Whether it's the first, second, or millionth dip, Jesus still loves you and doesn't want sin and wrong choices to keep you away from Him anymore.

I was speaking one time and said to the crowd, "How many of you are thankful that God gave you a second chance?" Everyone applauded with gratitude to God. Then I said, "How many thank God for a third chance?" Once again, they all clapped in agreement. Then I asked, "How many of you are grateful for a fourth chance? And a hundredth chance? And a MILLIONTH CHANCE?" I was trying to get the crowd to realize God's great grace that He's extended to us. It was a pretty good service. Afterward, this seventeen-year-old girl came and said, "I really liked your sermon, but I disagreed with one part." That's not what you look forward to hearing right after you speak. Trying to fight rolling my eyes, I decided to indulge her as I asked, "Oh really, which part?" She said, "The part about God giving us a second chance. And a hundredth chance, and a millionth chance." I asked, "What's wrong with that?" And she said, "Whenever God forgives, it's always the second chance because He forgot the last one!"

Oh man! That is so good. I looked at her and said, "You're speaking next week." I'm so thankful that whenever God forgives, it's always the second chance because He forgot the last one. God told us that He will take our sin and cast it into the depths of the sea (Micah 7:19). If God forgives and gave us that picture of throwing our sin into the depths of the sea, then stop going fishing! God goes on to say that He remembers our sin no more, once it's forgiven (Hebrews 8:12). So rest in His grace and serve Him now with a clear conscience.

Do you remember when Jesus asked Peter, "Do you love me more than these?" I bet you thought He was talking about the other guys on the beach. No. Jesus wasn't interested in starting another contest between them. So what else could "these" be? Are you ready for this? It's the fish!

How awkward are you now feeling for Peter? Here's Jesus—the King of kings, Lord of lords—asking Peter if he loved Him more than the fish. Why fish? This is what distracted Peter when he bailed on Jesus. Peter had left his fishing business to follow Jesus, but now we see that Peter had left his calling with Jesus to go back to fishing. He thought he was baiting the fish but the fish were really baiting him.

Here are some good questions, which I heard Joseph Stowell raise one time: What are the fish in your life? What lures you away from your calling? What's baiting you to bail? What is it, in the back of your mind, that tries to get you to give up? It may not even seem like it's necessarily bad, in and of itself, but has it become a distraction that is keeping Jesus from being priority number one? Maybe it's a destructive pattern in your life. It could be the lure of an affair. It could be anger or bitterness that you are refusing to let go of. I don't know. But God knows, and you know. In this moment, pause and simply tell Jesus, "I love You more than these." And you watch—as He welcomes you out of the dip and back to your calling again.

SECTION THREE

Chapter 8

YOU ARE HERE

My wife likes to shop. As a matter of fact, we all do in our family. When we go to the mall in our area, we know where everything is. The coffee shop we want to go to. The stores we want to look through, in that order. When we are traveling, however, and we happen upon a new mall, I resort to using my primal instincts to lead my family in unfamiliar and uncharted territory—hunting and gathering. (Just kidding—I grab my smartphone and take a quick photo of the mall map.)

You know what I'm talking about. You're in the middle of back-to-school shopping and everyone is way past the edge of hunger. You can smell the cinnamon pretzels far off, but you can't find the food court. The aroma is hanging in the air, teasing you. So what do you do? Exactly what I just said. You make your way to the illuminated map, and the first thing you do is find the little circle on the map that says, "You Are Here." Even in your state of hunger, you know you'll never find the pretzel place if you don't first know where you are right now. It's only after you discover where you are that you're able to see the steps leading where you want to go.

So many of us have had big dreams. Maybe you feel God has given you an amazing picture for your life. I love it when God opens a glimpse into His plan for our lives, but that excitement can quickly turn into frustration if we dive right into that plan without first understanding exactly where we are at the moment. If God gives a high school senior the dream to be a surgeon, he can't just go running toward a scalpel and bribe his friends to lie down on the table for him to practice. He has to first recognize that it's just the seed of a dream. Knowing where he is right now will help him determine the steps he needs to move toward that dream. If he circumvents this, that dream will die quickly…along with one of his practice patients!

You will never know how to go for the dreams and visions God has placed within your heart if you don't first carefully assess your "You Are Here" location.

You will never know how to go for the dreams and visions God has placed within your heart if you don't first carefully assess your "You Are Here" location. Otherwise you will find yourself in a dip of frustration and defeat. When this happens, God often comes to us and asks us a question to help us find ourselves again. It's the same question he posed to Adam and Eve: "Where are you?"

In the book of Genesis, there are two accounts that describe the beginning of humanity. The first story in the Bible is about creation, and the second story is about two trees. One tree was called the Tree of the Knowledge of Good and Evil; the other, the Tree of Life. God offered Adam and Eve access to all the trees in the garden, but they were not to touch the Tree of the Knowledge of Good and Evil. After a span of time, the devil appeared to them, and using the lure of the forbidden tree, he got their eyes on what they didn't have instead of what they did have. So they disobediently ate of the fruit, and immediately their eyes were opened in a way God never intended, and their hearts were flooded with shame as they realized they were naked. So they hid. They tried to hide from God. This is sad and funny at the same time.

In Genesis 3:9, God came looking for them and asked, "Where are you?" Now, whenever God asks a question, it's not because He doesn't know the answer. Daddy always knows. When our daughters were little, we would play hide-and-seek. They'd hide, but they were the worst hiders ever. They'd plop themselves down and sit on our floral-patterned couch while covering their eyes with their tiny, delicate hands. In a faint giggling voice, they'd squeak out, "You can't see me." And I, being the good father that I am, pretended not to be able to find them. Walking slowly in front of them sunk deep into the corners of the couch, I'd say in a goofy voice, "I wonder where the girls are!"

It was pretty silly for my girls to think they could hide from me. It's even sillier for us to think we can hide from God. He already knew where Adam and Eve were. The question was not for His benefit; it was for theirs. He was actually reaching out to Adam and asking, "Adam, what are you doing here? Do you know where you are?" No "You Are Here" was necessary for God, but He wanted Adam to be honest and confess where he was. Instead, Adam immediately started blaming everybody in the world, which at that time was a pretty limited number, really just God and Eve, but from his vantage point, he was blaming everybody in the world! Adam told God, "It's *this woman*—that *You* gave me."

It's interesting how, when we make a mistake, we are so quick to blame other people instead of taking responsibility for our own decisions. Instead of starting with our "You Are Here" reality and going from there, we turn it around to act like we had nothing to do with it.

Adam's reaction reminds me of a kid I once encountered at a church where I was preaching. Apparently he had gotten in serious trouble for something. I saw him sitting in the back with his hoodie pulled over his head, arms folded, and a scowl on his downcast face. At the end of the service, I walked over to him sulking in his chair and asked, "How are you doing?" He only responded with a quick jolt of his shoulders up and down as if to say, "I don't know."

I asked, "You mad?"

"Yeah."

"At who?" Again, the only response was the shoulder lift.

"You mad at your friends?"

"Yeah."

"You mad at your mom?"

"Yeah."

"You mad at God?"

A short pause. "Yeah."

Then I asked, "You mad at the devil?" He quickly turned to me with a confused look on his face that communicated, *What in the world are you talking about?*

I said, "Well, answer the question. Are you mad at the devil? Hasn't this even crossed your mind? The devil set a trap. You took the bait. You made a bad decision, you're in trouble, and now you're mad at God and everybody else. And not once has it occurred to you to be upset with the devil? That would be like me slapping you in the face and then pointing to a random stranger on the street and saying, 'He did it.'"

Why is it that when the devil tempts, distracts, and sets up a plan to get us in a dip, we turn around and shake our fist at God? He loves it when you don't know who the enemy is. God may be asking you today, "Where are you?" He doesn't need to know, but he wants *you* to know before He can get us to where we're supposed to be. Do you realize where you are and how you got there?

Adam responded, "We're naked, and so we hid." And God asked,

"Who told you?" Listen, even in your dip, God is passionately pursuing you, extending His hand to you, and asking, "Who told you to think differently about how I see you? Who told you to run from Me? What made you think that the answer was to hide instead of running back to Me?" There are far too many believers in hibernation, stagnation, and separation, all because they choose to hide rather than come running back to God.

STOP HIDING, AND REACH UP

I saw the greatest illustration of this in a mall. (Like I said, I spend a lot of time at malls.) As I was perched on one of my favorite benches, people-watching, I saw this father holding the hand of his toddler daughter. They were walking slowly through the main part of the mall that was busy with people walking in every direction. The little girl, distracted by all the bright colors in the windows of stores, let go of her father's hand and wandered off toward a particular store window. A few moments later, she reached back up to grab her father's hand once again. But it wasn't her father's hand this time. It was a complete stranger's. She didn't even notice at first.

Then, after a few seconds, this precious little girl looked up only to make this startling discovery. Eyes growing large, her little face panicked as she frantically scanned her surroundings for her father. He wasn't far away. He was just a few feet away, watching to see how she'd respond. Once the little girl locked eyes with her father, she began running to him. He stooped down, opened up his arms, and completely embraced his baby girl once again.

This is a great analogy of us. Unlike Adam, the little girl didn't try to hide from her father. She ran as fast as she could to him. Maybe you were close to your heavenly Father at one point, but you have since let go of His hand as the issues of life distracted you. And now you find yourself holding on to the hand of the world around you instead. Your heart is filled with panic. You feel lost and afraid.

Maybe you feel like God is a million miles away. Maybe you're in a dip and don't know how to climb out. But God is closer to you than that little girl's father was to her. And by first asking *where* you are, He is actually reminding you of *who* you are. He's asking more than, "Do you know where you are geographically?" He's asking, "How did you get here spiritually?" He's reminding you, "You're My child. When you feel lost, I don't write you off. I'm so close." Why would you hide when you feel lost? Why isolate yourself? When you remember who you are, how much God loves you, and how much grace God has for you, turn and run back to our heavenly Father. Just like the little girl, running into the arms of her dad.

By first asking *where* you are, He is actually reminding you of *who* you are.

The little girl in the mall ran boldly because she was so confident in her father's response. If you're not sure of God's response, then allow me to remind you that we can "come boldly to the throne of grace, that we may obtain mercy and find grace to help in the time of need" (Hebrews 4:16 NKJV). He will embrace you. Love you. Heal you. Forgive you. It's just the kind of Father He is, but we must seek Him with our whole hearts.

If you've been running, hiding, and avoiding God, it's time to return to the basics of who you are. Maybe right now you just need a starting point, where you can mark "I Am Here" on your map. Regardless of where "here" is, start there. If you're bitter, start there. If you've drifted a bit, start there. No matter how far you've wandered, start wherever you are. Even if you've totally turned your back on God, start there. And then reach up. Muster your courage to seek for His hand, which I promise is within reach, and come back to a life completely dependent on Jesus.

We usually find ourselves in the dip and ready to quit because we've forgotten, as Adam and Eve had, who we really are and whose we are. In an earlier chapter, we talked about the abundant life in John 10:10 for both now and in heaven. This is the abundant life God has always intended for us to live, and it is found when we are close to Him.

The Garden of Eden wasn't just for the external benefits like nature, food, animals, and all that it had to offer. More importantly, it was about a soul of dependence on God, which in turn would've produced a soul of abundance. It was the "more" we spoke about that is only found in a relationship with Jesus. Sometimes what you really need and what you've been looking for has been right in front of you the entire time.

As James W. Moore records in his book *The Power of a Story*, many years ago in South America, a crew of Peruvian sailors was sailing up the Amazon River, when they came upon a strange sight. A Spanish ship was at anchor in the middle of the water and all the crew members were lying on the deck. As the Peruvian sailors drew closer, they saw that the Spanish sailors were in serious trouble. They were in terrible physical condition. Their lips were parched and swollen. They were dying of thirst.

"Can we help you?" shouted the Peruvians.

The Spaniards cried out, "Water! Water! We need fresh water!"

The Peruvian sailors were confused and surprised by their request, and told them to lower their buckets and help themselves.

The Spaniards thought they were still in salt water, but they had crossed over into the mouth of the Amazon River and were anchored in fresh water for three days. They didn't discover it because they had given up and quit trying. They didn't realize that what they needed was right in front of them the entire time.

Adam and Eve disobeyed God, because they felt like there might be something else out there that could satisfy. The devil got their attention on what they didn't have instead of all they had right in front of them.

They had all they needed in their relationship with God and the Tree of Life. But they chose to hang on to the world, rather than to God. They were looking to be satisfied but searching in all the wrong places. I cheated on some tests in high school. But I never cheated off the kid who consistently got bad grades. Even if he offered, I said, "Nah…I'm good. I think I'll just guess." Why? Because you can't expect to find the right answers in the wrong places.

Maybe you've found yourself in a dip because you have been misled by thinking what you're looking for is somewhere outside of God's will. Some people think the answer is always somewhere else and so they start the hunt, but they're lacking clear directions because they've never established where their starting point is. They'll change churches. Change marriages. Change cities. Change schools. Change jobs. Maybe what you've been looking for has been right in front of you.

When you align your life with Jesus, be honest about where you are. Start with where you are. He'll help you. Run to Him as you're reminded of what you mean to Him. He will help you identify where you are so He can take you to where He wants you to go. He will reveal your purpose in Him and will take you to the dreams He's placed in your heart. Don't run from Him. Don't hide. Just look up and reach out. He's standing right there with open arms.

Chapter 9

OUT OF ORDER

One of the most intimidating rooms in the gym is the weight room. After walking through a wall of sweat as your initiation to belong in there, your eyes and ears are assaulted by all the people grunting and barking, lifting weights as though an Olympic gold medal depended on it. The strongest and shiniest are usually the dudes everyone is standing around, asking for advice about the newest protein shake and workout routine. I know this because that guy is usually me. Okay, I might be exaggerating a bit. Actually, it's never me. Nobody ever asks me for advice in the gym. But nevertheless, I go.

On one whole wall of this room you'll find the dumbbells. These free weights range anywhere from 5 pounds to 190 pounds, with the lightest weights on the left of the rack and the heaviest on the right. The placeholders for each dumbbell are clearly marked to help you know exactly where the weights should go. Every morning these weights are beautifully in order, but they never stay that way. By the time I work out in the evening, the 25-pound weights are in the 35-pound spots. The 55-pound weights are in the 45-pound spots. This happens every day.

How do all these weights get so out of order, every day? I'll tell you how. It happens when one person puts one weight in the wrong spot, and this triggers a domino effect for all the others. Because one weight is out of order, that leads to another weight going in another wrong spot. And another. And another. And another. For all those poor people who work out in the evening, like me, we have to hunt for matching weights, and let me tell you, it's very frustrating.

It's the same in life. We often find ourselves in a dip because one area got out of order. Which led to another. And another. And another. I spoke to a guy who claimed he was feeling far from God and didn't know why. So I inquired about a few things. "Are you praying?" He responded with his head down, "No." "Are you reading the Bible?" "No." "Are you in a small group of other believers where you encourage each other on a regular basis?" "No."

So, like the dumbbells at the gym, his priorities had gotten out of order. I encouraged him: "You've forgotten the basics and allowed things to get out of order, which brings confusion and the feeling like God is distant. But God didn't move. You did."

It's so easy for aspects of our lives to get out of order. We may start off focused and deliberate on doing first things first, but pretty soon Instagram invades the spot where we used to pray. Checking email goes in the spot where we used to read the Bible. And we stay home to binge-watch TV shows instead of getting in relationship with other believers in a small group. Or we stop attending church because we feel too tired on the weekend. We end up going through our entire day without acknowledging God and then wonder how things got so out of order.

In Psalm 37:23, God instructs us: "The steps of a good man are ordered by the Lord" (NKJV). Okay, if they really are ordered, then we need to find the order, because the order matters.

Are you in a dip because things have gotten out of order? Are your priorities out of whack? Has God slipped out of the picture? God fits only in first place, and when He's not, it affects everything else in our lives. Order matters. Jesus emphasizes this in Matthew 6:33 when he said, "Seek first the kingdom of God and His righteousness and all these things shall be added to you" (NKJV).

> Are your priorities out of whack?... God fits only in first place, and when He's not, it affects everything else in our lives.

We always expect everything to fall into place and *then* we'll put God first. It doesn't happen like that. God blesses where He's first. I want God to bless my day. So the very first thing I do when I wake up, with the temptation to go on my phone and check social media or email, is read the Bible for about fifteen minutes and then spend time talking with God. He blesses where He's first. Before an important meeting, I stop and pray under my breath, *God, I acknowledge you in this meeting. Please, give me wisdom and favor.* He blesses where He's first. My wife and I stop to pray when we're in an argument, which isn't easy to do if you're not used to this because you're more interested in being heard than understanding where your spouse is coming from. He blesses where He's first.

We expect to put God in third place or last and for us to still be blessed as if He were first. God knows that what you allow, you encourage. If God operated from disordered priorities, encouraging us to continue in destructive patterns, we would then think, *Oh, He blessed me over here and He's in eighth place. I guess He's good with that.* He's not. Let's not forget what's priority.

Think of student athletes. If they want to play sports, their grades must be priority. I was privileged to have a meeting with University of Alabama head football coach Nick Saban. He expressed, in a quiet voice of confusion, how disheartened he was over talented kids who could have a future in football if only they hadn't thrown it all away by not focusing on their education. They become more interested in partying than making school a priority, which then leads to them getting kicked off the team. Order matters.

It's funny, sometimes we know what we should be doing to get out of the dip, but because of pride we just don't. We would rather continue down a painful, out-of-order road, without God's blessing, instead of coming back to Him, putting Him first, and watching Him bless.

RESET

Here's the good news: if things are out of order for you right now, you can reset and start over. Growing up, I played video games. I'm not talking about the games out today. I'm not talking about these gaming systems with seventy-five buttons on the controller. I'm talking about the one and only original Nintendo Entertainment System. Are you old enough to remember the NES? Games like *Super Mario Bros*. Games like *Contra*. My favorite aspect of *Contra* was that it had a secret code to get thirty extra men. Some of you can still repeat the code in your mind right now. *Up, Up, Down, Down, Left, Right, Left, Right, B, A, Start!* Oh man! Those were the games. And back then, you couldn't sit anywhere you wanted in the living room. These controllers had cords. You had to sit on the floor, three feet away from the TV. And we loved it.

With today's games, it seems like it takes thirty minutes just for the game to start up. And when there's a glitch or you get stuck, you have to turn the entire system off and back on again, which takes another thirty minutes. Not with the old-school Nintendo. When you got stuck because of a glitch, all you had to do was reach down and blow on the game cartridge like a harmonica, or press a little button on the console that said RESET. Two seconds later, you were back up and running like new.

If you are reading this book, and you have allowed your life to get out of order, God has installed a reset button! In 1 John 1:9, we read this promise: "If we confess our sins, He is faithful and just and will forgive us our sins and cleanse us from all unrighteousness."

Asking for forgiveness looks like this: *God, I'm so sorry for going my own way. I confess I have allowed other things to come before You. Today, I'm reordering the list. Forgive me my sin and cleanse me. I'm putting You first again.* Be specific. Invite Him to be Lord again. Then He will do something that is almost unexplainable. When you reset the order, He resets your heart. Resets your life to the manufacturer settings. He makes you brand-new.

In the dip, we're looking for direction in life and feel so confused. When you reorder the list and make God first, He not only forgives and makes things new, but He also gives the directions you've been trying to find on your own.

THREE STEPS BACK TO ORDER

Instructions are important, but if you're like me, you often consider them to be optional. Several years ago, I bought some bunk beds for our daughters from IKEA. Weeellll, not *really* from IKEA. They were originally from IKEA, but I purchased them from someone else who bought them from IKEA. I had to go to their house, disassemble them, and then take them home to reassemble them without instructions. Now, I'm not the most mechanically inclined person. That's my brother, Chad. As a matter of fact, when our girls were growing up, anytime something broke in the house, they would say in their cute, patronizing voices, "Why don't you call Uncle Chad. I bet he can fix it." Yeah, that hurt as much as you think it did.

Well, not this time, Uncle Chad! I thought. *I will put these beds together myself. I'm a man!* Five hours later I was sweating. Dehydrated. Bewildered. *Why are there so many extra parts? Why do they have that one little screwdriver, or Allen wrench, or whatever you call it?* Somewhere in the world there are Swedish designers who created these IKEA bunk beds, eating their delicious Swedish meatballs and laughing. Laughing at how difficult they made it for me. And now I've got the weirdest-looking bunk beds you've ever seen.

I told the girls, "Come on in and see your new bunk beds!" They came rushing in with excitement only to have their look of excitement quickly change to confusion. One of them jumped on the top bunk at the precise moment when I realized that top bunk was not level. It was at a 30-degree incline, and the whole thing was way too high. When my daughter sat up from lying down, she hit her head on the ceiling. I know what you're thinking. I called my brother, Chad, to come fix it, right? Wrong. I called my brother-in-law. And *he* came over and fixed it. Take that, Chad. And IKEA!

> Many times when we try building without God's instructions, we are left with something not built to the specifications of its original design.

The point is many times when we try building without God's instructions, we are left with something not built to the specifications of its original design. In God's Word, He's given us instructions and has clearly communicated that He must be first. That order matters. Remember, God designed you and has a purpose for you, but we need to follow His instructions in His Word. In Proverbs, He has given us step-by-step instructions: "Trust in the Lord with all your heart and lean not on your own understanding; in all your ways submit to him, and he will make your paths straight" (3:5–6).

There are three steps here and one result. The problem is we want our paths to be made straight without following steps one through three.

If we refuse to follow the step-by-step instructions, our lives will end up looking like my daughters' IKEA bunk beds: slanted, out of balance, and unable to support the weight of life. So here's the correct order:

1. *Trust in the Lord with all of your heart.* Not some. Not a little bit. All of it. Put your full trust and dependence in Him.
2. *Don't lean on your own understanding.* Like me assembling the beds, don't think, *I got this.* Newsflash: we don't "got this" on our own. We need the Lord to help us get out of the dip.
3. *Submit to Him in all your ways.* Place Jesus at the center of your life. Like spokes on a bicycle wheel, the center will then touch every part of the tire. Place Jesus at the center of your life where He affects every area.

When we follow these steps, the good part comes next: *He will make our crooked paths straight.* In other words, He will direct you out of the dip. When you reorder the list and put God first, He gives the direction for your life that you have been searching for but have not been able to find.

I feel the Lord gave me a picture of this. I saw an asphalt road winding through hills in the countryside. You couldn't see parts of the road as it ducked behind some of the hills. So, if you were to look at the road ahead and try to see where it was leading, it would be very confusing. I saw the Lord, after we've done steps one through three, come over to the road and slowly lift it up and pop it, bringing it back down as one would do to straighten a carpet. That's what the Lord does. He can straighten out His path in front of you, even if our out-of-order lives have made our paths crooked. Could you use some more direction? Let Him guide you and make your paths straight. But remember that order matters. Put God first.

Chapter 10

A LID IN THE DIP

Remember when you were a kid and every idea seemed like a good one? My daughters always seem like they are inventing these good (or *great,* in their eyes) ideas. Several years ago, Dianna and I were going on a trip, and they wanted to go with us. Our second daughter, age four, had the bright idea for her older sister, age five, to hide inside one of our suitcases. Funny how most of these childhood "good" ideas usually require someone *else* to take the risk.

Our eldest folded herself into the suitcase while her sister slowly zipped the lid shut. Proud of her achievement, my daughter came to fetch me so I could revel in her genius. What she didn't realize, though, was that as she shut the door behind her, it locked. Sensing the click of the lock, she turned and tried the doorknob, which didn't budge. Instead of going to get me right away, she started panicking, trying to get back into the room. Pounding on the door, she began screaming for her sister.

Her older sister heard her cries and started panicking too. The only thing worse than panicking that your sister is in a suitcase in a locked room is being the sister who is locked in a suitcase in a locked room. This chaos went on for probably ten minutes. Can you imagine trying to extend your limbs inside a suitcase? Feeling your own hot breath against your face? Feeling claustrophobic?

Finally, the older sister, trapped in the suitcase, found her wits and had a thought that would lead to her breakthrough. In the darkness of the suitcase, she took her finger and searched for where the zipper began. She found a small opening where she poked her finger through and slowly slid the zipper all the way around in Houdini-like fashion, lifted the lid, and jumped out!

A lot of us have felt this way in life—hopefully, minus the suitcase. However, we all have seasons when we feel as if we are going through life with a lid over our heads. When our circumstances seem so much less than what we know is possible, and we don't believe we'll ever break free from them. Some of you might feel exactly like this right now. You have a dream that you want to believe will come true. You want so badly to reach it, and everything inside you desires to go for the John 10:10 life. But for some reason, this lid, this unseen opposition, is causing you to feel trapped and leading you to believe things will never be any different.

Maybe you don't think there's a way out because you've never seen anybody go beyond where you are. Maybe no one in your family has ever gone to college. Or no one in your family has ever been debt-free. Successful marriages are few and far between among family and friends. You're struggling to see a way to open that lid because you've never seen it done before. These scenarios can perpetuate a claustrophobic feeling, one that chokes out your faith, and you believe a John 10:10 life won't happen for you.

Maybe your lid presents itself in a different way. Insecurity hangs over your heart and mind like a heavy blanket. You can't shake an "I can't" mentality. Every time a suggestion is brought up, your immediate response is, "Oh, I can't do that." It's a lid. You have a wrong view of God and a wrong view of yourself. A feeling of insignificance or powerlessness is a lid. Anything that keeps you from growing any higher or experiencing anything greater is a lid.

So many of us think God might be able to use somebody *else* in another city, anybody other than us. That all those promises in the Bible are true for others, but probably not for me. God couldn't use *me* to start a business. Or write a book. Or make a difference in my generation. If we think this way, we put a lid over our thinking. Our lives are affected and directed by the way we think. If we want to live differently, then we have to think differently.

Our lives are affected and directed by the way we think. If we want to live differently, then we have to think differently.

Maybe, though, another person has placed a lid over your life. Someone at work may not believe in you, so you allow his or her words to shape the lid that will hover over your life, trapping you. So then you begin to isolate yourself from people because those negative words have dug so deeply into your heart that you don't want to put yourself out there again. We can't risk the humiliation and pain of someone saying something like that to us again. We isolate, and we insulate. You don't let anything in, even when it's God's voice through His Word or people trying to build you back up. Or maybe you see every suggestion or correction as an attack, so you turn around and weaponize it instead of growing from it, pushing people away. Stunting your own growth.

The problem with this approach to life is that God made us for relationship. Without people around us to help us grow, we box our lives into a suitcase and zip it shut. It's very difficult to trust again once you've been hurt; I know about this personally, but I've also had people build me up. Anytime I've ever grown, it's been with someone else putting their finger to my chest and saying, "You're better than this, Shaun.

Here's how you can grow. You're made for greatness." Anytime you've ever been blessed, it's been through people. A prayer. Encouragement. Provision. God loves to use people to bless people. So, if you're not in relationship with the right people, the view of your own insecurities and wrong people create the lid that will keep you from growing. Don't just gather around people who will tell you how great you are. Get around healthy believers who will stretch you to grow. Even when it's uncomfortable. God uses people to chisel away the ungodly things in our lives.

We all have lids in some area, and we need people around us to help. Me, myself, and I form an unhealthy small group. I'm willing to risk when it comes to relationships because the risk is worth it. The alternative is to quarantine. But no one has ever reached their destiny alone. We've toured Alcatraz, the infamous prison in San Francisco that was in use for many years. On the tour we were told that the worst place in that horrific prison was solitary confinement. People would go insane in isolation. We were not created to be alone.

Some people are boxed in because of shame from past failures. Let me give you a few words, and see if they accurately describe this feeling. You feel stuck, as if your tires are spinning in the mud and you're unable to go anywhere. You feel frustrated as you see where you want to be, but you've lost the faith that you can actually get there. You thought there was "more," but you have begun talking yourself out of believing God for more. This deep frustration has led to you feeling unable to change or achieve your goal. You're not making the impact you want to be making, or you haven't been as productive as you'd like. The people around you seem to be so much further along than you, and this almost indescribable, frustrating comparison game is boiling deep inside your soul. This is a dangerous progression because frustration never stays put; if not dealt with, it will always lead to hopelessness and despair.

Have guilt and shame created a lid over you? First, guilt slaps on a lid as it accuses you about what you've done. Then shame zips you up tight as it demeans who you *are*. Shame says there's no hope of you ever changing. You're boxed in. This is when you start accepting the dip and changing your address to 555 Dip Street. You think you're going to live in this place for the rest of your life.

If you find yourself in this place right now, let me encourage you. This is just a season; it's just a lid. And like my eldest daughter, who finally found a place to poke her hand through and slowly unzip herself to freedom, you too can pierce through the darkness and begin to believe God's Word is true and that you will experience once again—or for the first time ever—the John 10:10 abundant life!

LIDS

A lid, by definition, is "a removable or hinged cover" (per Dictionary .com).

READ THAT AGAIN. I want to make sure you catch it, because there's good news tucked inside that definition. It's removable! Meaning, as my friend and leadership expert John Maxwell so many times reminds us, "You can lift the lid!" There is hope that the lid can be removed. I don't care how long the lid has been over your life, and it doesn't matter how heavy you think it is. That lid can be removed, whether it be guilt and shame, or the negative words that have been spoken over you, or the weight of current circumstances. What I'm trying to say is, you're not as boxed in as you think.

It's time to lift the lid. There are people who are waiting for you to get out of the dip. People who need to know it can be done. People God has destined for you to impact. Even if you feel unqualified, you're in great company. There was a guy you might have heard of named Moses. God called him to do something he didn't feel qualified to accomplish.

> The Lord said, "I have indeed seen the misery of my people in Egypt. I have heard them crying out because of their slave drivers, and I am concerned about their suffering. So I have come down to rescue them from the hand of the Egyptians and to bring them up out of that land into a good and spacious land, a land flowing with milk and honey—[the Promised Land]...So now, go. I am sending you to Pharaoh to bring my people...out of Egypt." (Exodus 3:7–8, 10)

I love what we learn about God here. Notice what He spoke: First, "I've seen and heard." He is a God who sees us and hears our prayers. Always. Second, "I'm going to rescue." God not only sees us and hears our prayers, but He also responds and is faithful to rescue us out of any dip, large or small. Third, "I'm sending you." God chooses us. He chooses you and me to be His hands and feet and voice to do the rescuing!

But Moses wasn't buying it. He felt a huge, weighty lid over his life and leadership, one that he'd allow to hang over his head for years. But can we also cut this guy some slack and state the obvious here? How scary and intimidating would it be to waltz into Egypt, the superpower country during that time, and approach its leader, Pharaoh, and say, "Um, can you let your entire slave workforce go? Oh, and by the way, God told me to tell you. So, I'm not requesting, I'm demanding."

Moses was not looking at God's great plan at that moment. He only saw the lid. Then the excuses started flowing. How many times have we given excuses to God for why He shouldn't use us? In verse 11, Moses asked, "Who am I?" and God responded, "I'll be with you." Then Moses asked, "Who are You? Who do I say sent me?" God responded, "I am who I am." He's Almighty God. After that, Moses asked, "What if they don't listen?" Pressing God further, he insisted, "I'm not a good speaker." And finally, he just came out with what he'd been trying to say in his first four questions: "Just use someone else."

We look at Moses as someone who God used to do extraordinary things, but we sometimes forget that he wasn't that confident or secure a leader when God first called him. He was terrified. He was insecure. He was stuck in a dip and he had accepted the lid.

I can relate with Moses here because I know exactly what it feels like to think God has gotten me mixed up with someone else. I can take you backstage when I first started speaking and would be physically sick before coming out to preach at church every week. The insecurity and nervousness were so oppressive I wanted to run away. And my excuses started flowing. I might not have said it out loud, but I felt everything Moses had the guts to ask. Who am I? God, are you really with me? They're not going to listen to me. I can't speak like other people I've heard. Why did you pick me for this? Or *did* you pick me for this? Maybe I'm here, but misheard you and got it wrong that I should be doing this. Why don't you just use someone else? But like Moses, I had to step out even though I was afraid. Sometimes we just gotta do it afraid. God wanted Moses to engage in the fight, and He wants you and me to step out in faith too. We've got to stop wasting time panicking in the zipped-up suitcase, because we don't end up getting shipped to our destiny in a suitcase of uninvolvement. Remember how great God is and remember who you are in Him. Find your wits, and step out in faith.

I can relate with Moses here because I know exactly what it feels like to think God has gotten me mixed up with someone else.

ENOUGH WITH THE EXCUSES

God has heard the cry of the brokenness of our cities, just as He heard the Israelites cry out to him from the oppression of Egypt. He's seen the emptiness in people's lives as they attempt to fill themselves with things from the world that will never fulfill. He has a plan to rescue them and He wants to use you. Yes. You.

Enough with the excuses! We have to lift the lids because we will never fulfill God's plan for our lives inside that stifling suitcase. My daughter didn't have someone else lift the lid for her. She wanted to get out so badly that she did something. Stop waiting for someone else to do something. *You* do something. Don't be satisfied in the dip. Don't be satisfied in the darkness. Don't be content with living with this lingering lid over your life. Don't settle for a mediocre, mundane, suitcase mentality, with such a low expectation of your purpose in life.

Moses lifted the lid in his dip and grew into a great influencer. He grew into his purpose and was used by God to help so many others get out of their dip even though he was insecure in his. You can do the same. Stop with the excuses and be honest about where you are. If you are scared, tell God. If you're feeling stuck, frustrated, and deflated, tell Him. If you feel like you don't have what it takes, ask Him for wisdom. James 1:5 gives us a wonderful promise: "If anyone lacks wisdom, you should ask God, who gives generously to all without finding fault, and it will be given to you."

This verse means God will give you wisdom without pointing out all the reasons you don't deserve it. Since I was eighteen years old, I have prayed, *God, give me wisdom beyond my years. I know you've called me to great things that are so far beyond my own ability and I need You. Please grant me the wisdom I need to do what You've called me to do.* Maybe take a moment to stop right now and pray that same prayer over your life.

And then be determined to grow. You're called to be an influencer, and you don't have to become someone else to fulfill your purpose. Proverbs 12:24 tells us to "work hard and become a great leader" (NLT). Salvation is free, but becoming a leader is hard work; it requires you to do something. You can lift the lid, but it doesn't happen by itself. Take steps today to lift the lid, to rise above the dip, and walk into your destiny.

Working harder is about aiming in the right direction consistently. Fully dependent on Jesus and His Word. Relying on His empowerment and grace but taking the right steps, staying consistent even when you don't see much happening.

Today, right now, write down what you will specifically do from here. What's your next step? Maybe you need to enroll in college. Maybe you need to begin reading some leadership books and develop as a leader. Take seriously the position of influence God has placed you in. It could be that you need to sit down and write out a business plan for that dream in your heart. Maybe you need to join a church and get in a small group. Stop sitting on the sidelines. As our daughter reached over in the darkness of the suitcase, she was able to unzip the lid that was holding her down. She didn't make excuses and just stay there. She didn't even stay boxed in because she was so busy blaming her sister for putting her in the suitcase. She simply made the choice to get out.

At the end of the day, people are at stake. Lifting the lid is not just so you can feel better about yourself. We are here to reach people. We're here to make a difference in people's lives and fulfill God's purpose for our lives. In your business, at your church, with your family, at school. But in order for you to be effective in your purpose and make a difference in people's lives, it's going to require you to lift your lid.

Start. Start today. Start now. And be willing to learn from others. You can grow. You can make a difference. You don't have to accept the lid of limitations over your life. With God, all things truly are possible.

Chapter 11

DON'T SETTLE

I was on a laser-focused mission with my taste buds as my compass. It was a late night in Los Angeles, where Dianna and I had just been involved in several meetings, and we were tired and hungry. Correction. We were *HANGRY*. Far past the point of dinner. Having a very specific culinary experience in mind, I was on the hunt and would settle for nothing less than the perfect will of God.

Dianna? Not so much. After an hour of driving through the congested maze that is Los Angeles, not to mention passing up some very acceptable restaurants, she got so frustrated that she finally blurted out, "Shaun! Enough already! Just pick something. Anything. I'm so tired. Let's just get fast food." I wonder how many spouses can relate. I wanted to find the very best, but Dianna was so worn out, tired, and hungry she was willing to settle for anything.

When it comes to food, settling for a meal or two is no big deal. You can eat fast food a couple times a month and still stay pretty healthy. However, a lifestyle of fast food will put you in the hospital. And so it is with our lives. We need to be careful about making "fast food" decisions when we're tired, or frustrated, or feeling defeated, because we might just settle for anything—instead of holding out for God's best. God has a best, but mediocrity always seems reasonable when you doubt God's best. Tell yourself right now, *I'm not going to settle*. Do not settle for the thought that God is to be seen from a distance but not experienced. Do not believe the lie that this is all there is in life. God has more available. But He needs you to not settle and to never quit in the dip.

There's a story in chapter 32 of the book of Numbers, where we read about a group of people, an entire nation, who had settled. The backstory is that God's people, the Israelites, had been in slavery for four hundred years to the Pharaoh, in Egypt. The people cried out to God for a deliverer, and God sent a man named Moses. And through a series of miraculous events, God set his people free.

Can you imagine what that day must have been like as the Israelites experienced a new reality, which former generations had stopped believing in or even dreaming about? Some cried in utter amazement. Others laughed and danced and sang as they left the life of slavery and headed toward freedom! But whenever God calls you out of something, He also calls you into something. It was not enough to simply come out of bondage; God wanted to take them into a blessing. As His people walked out of Egypt, God directed them to Canaan—the Promised Land.

Whenever God calls you out of something, He also calls you into something.

With all the excitement and awe among the people, they made their way to the precipice of the Promised Land, which would have been about a fourteen-day journey. They probably celebrated the entire way. They were so elated and overwhelmed about the endless possibilities of a new and better life—that is, until they arrived outside the Promised Land and realized it was not currently available. There were others occupying the land.

They sent twelve spies to check out the land, and when they returned with their report, only Joshua and Caleb said, "We can do this." Only two of the twelve. The other ten said, "There's no way! Those people in there are huge. I don't know what they're feeding those Canaanites, but they are massive giants and we're like grasshoppers in comparison."

Not only did these ten have a bad view of themselves, but they also had a bad view of God. Isn't it funny how quickly we forget the incredible miracles God has done for us and how easily we are intimidated into quitting? Remember, this is right after God's amazing rescue. God moves in our lives mightily, but then we somehow lose the faith to believe Him for more. It's wild how willing we are to settle because we are afraid to believe God.

Doubt began to spread among the congregation of people who, just two weeks prior, had seen God do the impossible. They had experienced the miraculous but were now deathly afraid. Instead of being willing to follow God, they settled for smiling and waving at the music truck—even though God had promised a freezer filled with milk-and-honey ice-cream sandwiches.

By the way, the people who lost faith were not your average Israelites. These were leaders of tribes! But they didn't believe God was bigger than the problem in front of them. Listen, our lives are affected and directed by the way we think. And the way we think determines the way we live.

Their thoughts following a negative report affected and infected an entire congregation. Why? Because negative reports are contagious, and they often make it seem sensible to stay put. To settle in the dip. It's always easier, in our minds, to quit in the dip. But that's not what God had for them. Pretty soon, they were talking about killing Joshua and Caleb for believing the God who brought them out of slavery. Now everyone was saying, "It cannot be done."

So God says, "Fine. Because of your murmuring, complaining, and unbelief, you can just wander around in the wilderness." And that

Israelite generation would indeed wander in the wilderness for forty long years until everyone from that generation died in the desert, save Joshua and Caleb. Remember, there is God's way, and there is your way—but our way always leads us into a wilderness. There are no other options. Many of us have found ourselves in a wilderness, a dry place spiritually, because we, too, are very acquainted with the harsh reality that we chose to settle instead of stepping into God's preferred plan. When we are living outside of God's plan, we end up missing out on what God has for us.

If we fast-forward to Numbers 32, the Israelites prepared to enter the Promised Land for the second time. After all those years. This would have been around year thirty-nine of the forty years of wandering. They were children the first time they were here. They had dreamed of this moment. They had sung songs about this moment. They had told stories about this moment and now they were finally here. How long did they wonder what it would be like to have a home, and what it would be like to enter into what God had for them? Their dreams were about to become a reality.

There were twelve tribes of Israel. As they began to move as one into what God had promised them, Scripture reveals some who still were not ready:

> [The tribes of Reuben and Gad], who had very large herds and flocks, saw that the lands of Jazer and Gilead were suitable for livestock. So they came to Moses and Eleazar the priest and to the leaders of the community, and said…"The land the Lord subdued before the people of Israel—are suitable for livestock, and your servants have livestock. If we have found favor in your eyes," they said, "let this land be given to your servants as our possession. Do not make us cross the Jordan." (Numbers 32:1–5)

At this, Moses got furious. He said, "This is exactly what your forefathers did forty years ago. That's why we have been wandering around here in the desert. And now we are at the edge of the Promised Land and you are going to do the same thing? Have you not learned anything?"

They responded: "For we will not inherit with them on the other side of the Jordan, because our inheritance has fallen to us on the east side of the Jordan" (Numbers 32:19).

How many times have we tried to decide where our inheritance ought to be instead of where God has told us it should be? Let's have a short quiz: Where were they supposed to go? Canaan, the Promised Land. Where did God say their inheritance was supposed to be? Canaan, the Promised Land. The tribe of Gad knew that, and heard that, and still said, "I know God has more for us. I know this isn't His plan. I know it's not God's will, but we choose to stay on this side of the Jordan instead of crossing over into the Promised Land. Instead of obeying God. Instead of following God into His full blessing. We'd like to just stay over here."

What's scary is that God gave them their request! Sometimes, God will give you what you ask for even though it is not His perfect will. "So Moses gave Gilead to [them], and they *settled* there" (Numbers 32:40, emphasis mine).

They settled. Why did they settle? I suppose there could be several reasons why they settled. It may resemble the same reasons why we settle and do not believe God for more. Sometimes we settle because we are just tired. In their defense, they had been traveling for a long time. They had a lot of sheep. They had been wandering around with screaming kids asking, "Are we there yet? Are we there yet? I have to go to the bathroom." And the dad was saying, "You should have gone back at the last cactus. I'm not stopping again." Can you imagine traveling in the wilderness for that long? Aimless wandering.

They had grown tired. And they knew that to keep on going meant they would have to expend more time, more energy, more battles—and so they looked around at where they were, and they said, "This land is suitable" (see Numbers 32:1). Translation: "It'll do."

Do you know that when you get tired, your judgment is thrown off? Like Dianna and me looking for that restaurant. Fatigue led to frustration, which led to settling for something inferior. When you're worn out, it's easy to look around and react as the people of Reuben and Gad did, saying, "This will do. I'm too tired to go on," instead of following God all the way to the destination He intended for you.

Do you know the number one answer to the question "How are you doing?" is "I'm tired"? If that is you, let me encourage you. You are not alone. Galatians 6:9 encourages us: "Let us not become weary in doing good, for at the proper time we will reap a harvest if we do not give up." Harvest comes to those who do not give up. We all get tired, but do not let the desire for relaxation rob you of the joy of God's promise.

> Do you not know? Have you not heard? The Lord is the everlasting God, the Creator of the ends of the earth. He will not grow tired or weary, and his understanding no one can fathom. He gives strength to the weary and increases the power of the weak. Even youths grow tired and weary, and young men stumble and fall; but those who hope in the Lord will renew their strength. They will soar on wings like eagles; they will run and not grow weary, they will walk and not be faint. (Isaiah 40:28–31)

Don't give up. I heard a story one time of a married couple. The wife fell into a coma and the husband stayed by her side for days. Days turned into weeks. Weeks into months. Finally, the man grew so tired and depressed that he took his own life, only to have his wife wake up from the coma a week later.

Don't quit. Don't give up. Don't settle. Too many people give up on life too early and miss what God really has for them. Don't be another statistic. God has more for you. Don't let fatigue make you bail out on God's promise just because it's taking longer than you expected.

AVOID THE DISTRACTIONS

Sometimes we settle because we get tired, and other times we settle because we get distracted. That's why it is so important to keep vision in front of us. "Where there is no vision, the people perish" (Proverbs 29:18 KJV).

You may have heard the phrase "vision leaks." That means that we can get inspired, but if we do not constantly feed that in our lives, pretty soon our desire to see it accomplished dissipates. And where we once were so excited, we have now grown comfortable and we settle. Distraction is a huge weapon the devil uses to get us to settle.

Numbers 32:1 tells us why this group of people got distracted: they had very large herds. That's why they said, "Let's stay in Gilead and not go into the Promised Land." I wish I had been there to ask them, "Where did you get these large herds?" If you read the previous chapters, you discover they acquired them from recent battles where God had given them the victory. God blessed them, and now that blessing was keeping them from where God wanted them to go. God wants to bless you. The question is not, "Does God want to bless me?" The question is, "Can I handle the blessing of God when it comes?" Or "Will that blessing turn into a stumbling block that will keep me from following God in the future?"

They settled in the dip because they were distracted. They thought, *What are we going to do with these herds? It's going to be a lot of work to get all these animals over into the Promised Land. We think it would be better if we just stayed over here. This looks good enough.* It may have looked good, but it was not the Promised Land. It was not what God had for them.

Earlier in their journey, the devil had tried to get them to revolt and return to where they had come from: "They said to each other, 'We should choose a leader and go back to Egypt'" (Numbers 14:4). Really? I can't believe that was even a consideration. We look at this and ask, "Was that really on the table? Y'all were considering going back to the whips and the slavery and the brick-making and the bondage? Are you kidding me? Are you really saying this was an option?" We look at them and can't believe that they were entertaining this, but the devil does the same thing to us today.

Have you noticed how he tries to get you so tired and distracted that he entices you to go back to what God has brought you out of? He'll remind you of the good times you had, but he will never remind you of the emptiness and the tears of desperation you experienced, crying out to God, saying, "God, if you're real, please get me out of this!" And He comes through, but then after a span of time you start entertaining thoughts of going back. Do not glorify your past. Remember what God has brought you out of and live a life of thanksgiving for all He has done to set you free.

Remember what God has brought you out of and live a life of thanksgiving for all He has done to set you free.

Thank God the Israelites did not go back in Numbers 14, but in chapter 32 the devil basically says, "I can't get them to go back into bondage, so I'll just try to convince them to not go any further." He wanted anything for them but the Promised Land. "Go back or stay here, but just do not go into what God has for you." The enemy is scared for you to obey God, because he knows he loses if you do. He's not afraid of who you are; he's afraid of who you might become. So he will try distracting you in order to get you to settle. I've heard that there are even more accidents caused by distracted driving than drunk driving. So many people are driving on life's freeway distracted. No wonder people are crashing in life. When we lose sight of God's purpose, we get distracted by the devil's schemes. And so these two tribes stayed in the city of Gilead instead of going into God's Promised Land.

God really does have more for you. God has a Canaan for you. Don't try and decorate Gilead like Canaan. He has a Promised Land for you. God has a plan and a destiny for your life. This is not the time to quit. This is not the time to get spiritual ADD. Do not get distracted. Do not disengage. Stay focused on what God has for you, because God's promise is even better than Gilead.

DON'T LOSE HOPE

Winston Churchill is believed to have said, "Success is going from failure to failure without a loss of enthusiasm." Don't quit. Keep going! Some people settle because they simply lose hope. The tribe of Gad wanted to stay on the east side of the Jordan instead of crossing over. They claimed that Gilead was their inheritance. But *Gad's* inheritance was not *God's* inheritance. Think about it: to have come so far after walking in the desert for forty years, waiting, dreaming, anticipating, longing for more…but then settling on the edge of God's promise being fulfilled. They came so close. They would've been able to see the Promised Land from their doorstep. From their windows, they were probably able to hear the sounds of those who reached the Promised Land celebrating. But they chose to settle. They quit too early.

Maybe you were once hopeful, but then something changed. Maybe you have recently been talking yourself out of believing God, saying things like, "I'm too old" or "I'm too young" or "I'm too busy" or "I'm too damaged." There is hope for you.

> For in this hope we were saved. But hope that is seen is no hope at all. Who hopes for what they already have? But if we hope

> for what we do not yet have, we wait for it patiently. (Romans 8:24–25)

> Be joyful in hope, patient in affliction, faithful in prayer. (Romans 12:12)

> May the God of hope fill you with all joy and peace as you trust in him, so that you may overflow with hope by the power of the Holy Spirit. (Romans 15:13)

Let me give you three points. All three are life-changers. Are you ready for them?

1. Don't settle. Trust God for more. Believe God for more. Follow Him with all of your heart. Walk in full obedience with total surrender and do not settle for anything less than God's best for your life.

You'll want to circle this next one:

2. Don't settle. You *can* have vision for your future. You can know purpose. Life doesn't have to be meaningless and hopeless. In a relationship with Jesus, you can have the abundant life Jesus came to bring, where we look forward to our life with Him in heaven one day and enjoy His presence and purpose on earth today.

Now, don't miss this last point:

3. Don't settle! I know what you're thinking: *Did Shaun make a mistake by making all the points the same point?* No. I'm trying to emphasize how mission critical it is for you not to settle.

Because...Yes! There is more to life! Yes! You can have more, but the "more" you've been looking for is found in no other place than our Promised Land: our relationship with Jesus Christ. Let's be people who don't just sit back and watch other people walk into their destiny or stop short of what God has for us. But let's walk all the way into His promise.

I know you're frustrated in the dip right now, but this is my prayer for you:

> *God, I'm asking for my friend reading this book right now that they not settle for anything less than Your best. I know they're tired. I know they might be distracted, but I pray that You restore hope in them now. I'm asking that You help them not to quit in the dip and not to settle. Let them, through this book, see Your grace and the amazing promises You have for them in Your Word. In Jesus' name, amen.*

SECTION FOUR

Chapter 12

THE SECRET OF KNOWING

People do some crazy things if they think there's a benefit. They'll drink juiced vegetables with wheatgrass because they believe in the health benefits. It's not because it tastes good. It doesn't. It tastes like turtle spit. But health fanatics drink the turtle spit faithfully, even investing in their own personal juicers, because they see the benefit. They'll exercise instead of sitting on the couch with a plate full of cookies, not because they enjoy manual labor, but because they see the benefit.

People will eat salads instead of chocolate molten lava cakes because they see the benefit. Personally, I see plenty of health benefits from lava cake: antioxidants from the dark chocolate. Chocolate comes from cocoa beans. Which is a plant. And salad is a plant. So, chocolate is basically like eating a salad. I think you get the point. When we see the benefit of something, we will do the work to attain the prize.

James, the half brother of Jesus, understood this concept when he wrote a letter to the twelve tribes of Christians scattered all over because of severe persecution for their faith. These Christ followers had been on the run, scared for their lives, living in caves. They were desperately awaiting word from Jerusalem to let them know they could come home. It was rough. It was painful. These refugees were in need of a fresh word that would bring a message of hope for their present situation.

Then James wrote a letter and sent it to all of them. I can only imagine their excitement when they received word from this leader of the Jerusalem church. They were probably expecting and anticipating James to proclaim, "The persecution has subsided! You can come on home now!" Imagine their huge disappointment when they opened the letter and it started off with this:

> Consider it pure joy, my brothers and sisters, whenever you face trials of many kinds, because you know that the testing of your faith produces perseverance. Let perseverance finish its work so that you may be mature and complete, not lacking anything. (James 1:2–4)

When going through trials, count it *pure joy*? Umm…excuse me? That's not what they wanted to hear. There's *more* testing to take place? Are you kidding me? After crowding together and living in caves, they wanted to hear that the coast was clear. We're not much different from them, are we? We don't love to be tested, nor do we naturally find joy in it.

We don't want to go through the work of it when we simply cannot see the benefit. In fact, we even say things like, "Don't test me." Maybe you've said this before to someone who *knows* what they're about to do will drive you crazy, and you warn, "Don't you test me!" It means, "Don't you push me to my limit." We may say that to other people in moments of frustration when they are pushing our buttons. We have gotten so familiar with this response, though, that we often turn around and unfortunately use the same mentality with God. We look at God and say, "Don't You test me, God. Don't You push me to my limit." Maybe we don't say it out loud, because we're far too Christian to actually say it, but we think it…forgetting that God knows our thoughts before we even think them. Why do we have this attitude? Because we have forgotten that there are certain benefits and life lessons that cannot be achieved any other way. In these moments, I know we don't see any benefit, but sometimes we need to drink the turtle spit because eventually there will be a benefit.

DO TEST ME!

Let's camp out here for a moment and unpack this together. When James said, "Count it all joy," he wasn't talking about a feeling. Our feelings are fickle; one minute they are up, and the next they are down. In addition, the littlest things in life can affect whether we are happy or not. We're happy about our job because they have cake in the breakroom; then we're sad about our job because our boss asked us to stay late. We're happy because we found the clearance rack in our favorite department store, but then we're sad because we cannot find our size. We're happy, we're sad, and it can change in a second. James chose this word *joy* because joy is not the same as happiness. Happiness is based on happenings, or whether or not things are going well. Joy is not a feeling. It's a benefit *and* a choice. Joy doesn't depend upon outward circumstances. Happiness comes and goes. But joy is made up of something entirely different than happiness. It's consistent. It's a spiritual strength and an unwavering confidence that God is in control.

Nehemiah points out that "the joy of the Lord is your strength" (8:10). When you lose your strength, that's a good sign that you've lost your joy. There are a lot of joyless believers walking around because they've confused joy with happiness and happenings. They feel empty because they had to walk through difficulty, and it zapped their strength.

James is teaching us that just because we're walking through a dip doesn't mean God is not with us. Quite the opposite: the dip can actually be used to do something in you. In other words, testing can bring growth.

Notice James did not say *if* you face trials, but *when* you face them. Every person has a dip. Every person gets tested in life. So when you do, count it pure joy. Count it all joy, because there's a benefit. The test will most certainly come, and it's up to you to count it as joy and to learn the lesson in the dip. Why? Because "you know that the testing of your faith produces perseverance" (James 1:3). The test is producing the *perseverance* you need for your next step. Don't just skim by that concept. Let it sink in. No one likes a trial, *but* we can still have joy in that trial if we know it will produce something that cannot be achieved any other way. Trials are what produce and develop perseverance. In other words, there can be development in the dip. You can hate the circumstances, but still count your trial as joy, learn in the dip, and when you come out you will say, "I've grown so much because of what that test developed in me."

No one likes a trial, *but* we can still have joy in that trial if we know it will produce something that cannot be achieved any other way.

Every great man and woman of God has had a season of testing and preparation. Joseph had thirteen years of testing. Moses had a desert. Esther had the threat of Haman and the annihilation of her people. The three Hebrew boys had a fiery furnace. Daniel had a lion's den. David had Goliath. Paul was called by God and then spent three years in caves learning. Even Jesus was publicly affirmed by the heavenly Father, and then went immediately into the wilderness where Satan himself tested and tempted Jesus.

If all of these people, whom God used to do the greatest things, had to go through a season of preparation, what makes you think you get to bypass the very thing that's preparing you for greatness? Let God work! Embrace the secret of knowing that the test is producing something in you to get you ready for your next season.

C'S GET DEGREES

Did you ever try and make up an excuse to get out of a test in school? Do you remember sitting down to a test, skimming through the questions on the paper, and thinking, *I'm in trouble*?

If the test was multiple choice, like one of those Scantron tests, I knew I was in trouble. I hated those tests. When I'd read option A, I'd think that sounded right. Until I read option B and thought, "Well, B sounds good too." And then I'd read option C and think, "It could be C." I found myself more times than not just filling in the circle for option D: All of the above. When my teacher said those dreadful words, "Time's up, pencils down," in a panic I'd quickly fill in the rest of the answers...ABACADABA all the way down and hope for the best.

There's a saying in college that goes, "Cs get degrees." In other words, as long as you pass, you can still get the degree, so it's fine to just barely get by. Do the bare minimum to pass because it doesn't matter if you learn or not; you just need the degree. This is a very different mentality than knowing the test is producing something in you and preparing you for your next season. I don't know about you, but if I need surgery, I don't want a doctor who barely passed; I want the best doctor who actually learned everything he or she needed to in medical school.

We're missing the point when we have a "Cs get degrees" mentality! There are tests that God uses to promote us. How can we expect promotion if we reject God's curriculum? Not everybody makes it to their destiny. Let that sink in for a second. There are those in life who get worried and drop out of their destiny. There are others who get distracted and fail. Others don't believe they'll ever see the benefit, so they don't place any value on what they learn. Everybody doesn't make it to their destiny, but *you* can! You will when you begin to embrace the test and learn—in the dip—what God is trying to teach you in preparation for the next step.

God is the greatest teacher, and He loves to watch you succeed. He doesn't want to see you fail. God doesn't want you to just fly through life and barely receive a passing grade. He wants you to learn what He's trying to teach you and to get prepared for what's coming next.

There was a time when our daughters would cry about doing their schoolwork. They'd say, "Dad, why do we have to learn this? We're not even going to use this stuff." Then they'd look at me and inquire, "Do you use fractions?" And my response was brilliant at first: "Uh, not really." And you know the question coming after this one: "Then why do we have to learn it?" I was almost stuck, but then my parenting skills kicked in. Parents, I'm going to help you with this argument. Are you ready? My response to their question was, "To get to the next level." Boom! You're welcome.

You don't have to fully understand God to fully obey Him. Mary, the mother of Jesus, didn't have to fully understand in order to fully obey. Faith is not about knowing the how. It's about obeying the Who and the what. Which is God and His Word.

You don't have to fully understand God to fully obey Him.

Don't get worried and drop out. Don't quit on the dream when you're so close. Don't get distracted and fail. I'm trying to get you to see the benefit in the test so you value what you're learning. Tests help lead you into a new season. Graduation. Promotion. Advancement. No one simply arrives. John Maxwell once told me, "No one ever quit their way to the top." Let's make a pact to never quit in the dip!

IN THE MEANTIME

In Genesis, Joseph went through some tests. Probably way more tests than he wanted. He was betrayed. Human trafficked. Falsely accused. Thrown in prison for something he didn't do. And finally, he was forgotten. We'll unpack much more of Joseph's story in a later chapter, but right now let's just focus on the testing aspect of his life. Psalm 105:18–19 (NKJV) explains, "They hurt his feet with fetters, He was laid in irons. Until the time that his word came to pass, the word of the LORD tested him."

Joseph had a prophetic dream when he was seventeen years old, but that dream wouldn't come to pass for another thirteen or so years. Although Joseph would eventually be elevated to second in command of Egypt, as a teenager he was not nearly ready for this world-changing post. He needed to learn and mature in both wisdom and character, and the way he achieved this was through the many tests he passed. As Psalm 105 states, "The word of the LORD tested him" until Joseph was fully prepared for the time when his calling and future could come to pass.

Only because Joseph embraced the tests with excellence, as opposed to the "Cs get degrees" mentality, was God able to elevate him to become second in command of the most powerful nation of the world. Through him, thousands of people's lives were saved, and he never would have been able to arrive at his destiny if he hadn't learned from the tests along the way. Are you catching this? You can go through the test if you *know* that it's producing something to help you get to where God wants to take you. Just because you don't see the benefit doesn't mean the benefit will not eventually be seen. A popular saying is, "Seeing is believing," but for Christians, "Believing is seeing" is just as true.

BRING THE HEAT

It's crazy how fast clothes get wrinkled. The moment you put on a shirt, the "wrinklage" begins. The front. The back. The arms. Little creases all over. Sometimes you'll see a person's shirt that's way too neat, without any wrinkles whatsoever. They show up like, "Hey, guys, I woke up like this." But you're on to them. You know the real truth and how they managed that because you've done the same thing: you carefully climb into the car and put your seat belt on, and with one hand, you hold out the seat belt by an entire arm's length. If you got in an accident, you'd fly into the air, but your shirt would be wrinkle-free.

Let me paint you a picture to help you see the point. We all fall into one of three categories when it comes to wrinkles in our clothes. One, some don't care. Two, some don't see. Three, some don't know.

One: some don't care. They're wrinkled, and they couldn't care less. They've got more important things to think about. This is not a priority for them. What have a few wrinkles ever done to hurt anybody? Besides, some of us have learned a little secret. When you're in a hurry, we've figured out how to iron only the front of the shirt and then wear a jacket over it. So while you look good from the front, you really are a wrinkled mess! But our image is smooth and we're really only concerned about the part of us that people see. Are you catching the analogy?

Two: some don't see. They're wrinkled but they genuinely don't notice their shirt is a crunched-up wreck. And they don't have anyone close enough to them to tell them, "Hey, maybe you should iron that shirt before you go into the job interview." In the same way, we all need a small group of people around us who can help point us in the right direction when we don't see the wrinkly issues in our life. We need people who can call out our blind spots.

Three: some don't know. They have never been taught how to get the wrinkles out. They don't know how to plug an iron in, let alone use it. It's not that they don't see the wrinkles. They do. It's not that they don't care. They do. They just don't know how to get them out. Maybe they're afraid to ask. Maybe they have gone so long not knowing that they are too embarrassed to ask.

We all fall into one of these three categories when it comes to issues in our life. There are some of us who don't care. Some who don't see. And some who don't know how to deal with them. Let me draw the connection between the wrinkles in our clothes and the wrinkles in our life.

What's interesting about wrinkles in our clothes is I can't just wave my hand over the shirt and wipe the wrinkles away. No, I have to take it over to an ironing board, and lay it down flat. Interesting side note: Psalm 23 says, "The Lord is my shepherd, I lack nothing. He *makes me lie down* in green pastures." Sometimes we have to be made to lie down so God can get our attention and begin to iron out some wrinkles in us.

Back to the shirt. I take the shirt and lay it down on the ironing board. I grab the iron and turn it on. By the way, don't you think it's funny how irons have different settings? I don't know why because I've only ever used one setting: high!

I then apply the weight of the iron. But not *just* the weight—I also apply the heat. But not *just* the heat—I add some steam. This is not a fast process. It's only after I've applied the weight, the heat, and the steam that I am able to get *some* of the wrinkles out.

God sees the wrinkles in our life and wants to help iron them out. Ephesians 5:25–27 tells us, "Christ loved the church and gave himself up for her to make her holy, cleansing her by the washing with water through the word, and to present her to himself as a radiant church, *without stain or wrinkle*" (emphasis added).

Did you read that last part? "Without stain or wrinkle." Aren't you grateful to Jesus that He can wash us clean *and* get the wrinkles out?

Now, I've tried to get *all* the wrinkles out of my clothes. But it seems impossible on my own. It's actually not until I take my shirt to the cleaners, the professionals, that they're able to apply more weight than I could apply on my own, more heat than I could on my own, and more steam than I could on my own. Then and only then are they able to present me with a shirt that is truly wrinkle-free.

In life, we're incapable of getting all the wrinkles out on our own. That's why we need Jesus. He's the ultimate cleaners. If He were to open a cleaners near you, it would be called "Without Stain or Wrinkle Cleaners," because not only is He able to remove every stain, but He also knows how to iron out every wrinkle. Some of us come to God and we're excited that our stains are gone but then we fight Him when He tries to iron out the wrinkles.

Salvation is when Jesus washes us clean and forgives our sin. But you can be saved and still have wrinkles. You can be a Christ follower and still have issues. James tells us how to get the wrinkles out. "Consider it pure joy, my brothers and sisters, whenever you face trials of many kinds, because you know that the testing of your faith produces perseverance. Let perseverance finish its work so that you may be mature and complete, not lacking anything" (James 1:2–4).

Tests and trials are the heat that God allows in our lives in order to iron out the wrinkles. He wants you mature and complete. But that doesn't just happen. There's a process for everything in life and we understand that.

In the dip, in the test, don't believe for a minute that it's for nothing. When you are submitted to God, it's building you up for something. It's preparing you for something. It's getting you ready for something that you cannot handle right now. James said the testing produces perseverance. Endurance. One translation says patience. Listen. Just because you're waiting doesn't mean you're patient. You need patience and endurance in order to trust the process. Let God iron out the wrinkles. Notice

James adds, "Let perseverance *finish* its work..." How many people never make it to their destiny because they won't let God finish? Let God finish building perseverance in your life so that you can truly be "mature and complete, not lacking anything." We all want to be mature and complete and lack nothing, but we don't want a test. It's like I hate flying but I love getting to the destination. I want the destination without the flight. We want the result without the process. But that's not how this works. You can make it by keeping your eye on the benefit because the benefit will far outweigh the test. Drink the turtle spit. I promise you, the joy of completing the test far outweighs the temporary discomfort of the test. God is training you in a storm for post-storm opportunities.

In the dip, in the test, don't believe for a minute that it's for nothing. When you are submitted to God, it's building you up for something.

Chapter 13

GOD USES EVERYTHING

It's 11:45 p.m. Your stomach is rumbling. The pangs of hunger are so loud you know you're not going to sleep. All you can think is, *I have to get up and get a late-night snack.* Slowly and quietly, so as not to rouse anyone, you sneak to the kitchen, grab a spoon, open the cupboard door, and reach for the bag of flour. A cloud of flour fills the air as you dive your spoon into the bag, lift it to your mouth, and take the biggest, most satisfying bite ever. "This is so good!" said no one ever! No one has ever said, "I sure am thirsty. You know what I could go for? A mug of vanilla extract or, better yet, maybe a whole bottle of cooking oil." No one has ever craved an entire carton of salt. No one has ever sat on the couch watching a movie while eating a tub of baking soda.

I think we can all agree that not one of these foods would be enjoyable alone. But it's amazing what happens when you take all of these ingredients and mix them together in a bowl. Something happens in the process. There's a blending that takes place. And then there's something even greater that happens when you take all these mixed ingredients and put them in some heat. Three hundred fifty degrees, for about thirty minutes. Something happens to the molecular structure. That which once was flat begins to rise. The bitter is overtaken by the sweet. And if you leave it in the heat long enough, you have something so delicious people will line up just to take a bite.

In the same way, if you isolate the events in your life, there are probably several that wouldn't be enjoyable alone. They were painful. Hurtful. Bitter. Abrasive. No one gets married with the hopes of a divorce. No one chooses to lose a job or get bullied at school. These isolated events, as with most individual ingredients, are not enjoyable. In addition, when we hunger for fulfilling destinies, negative experiences are not the ingredients we would pick to help get us there. But a master chef knows how to take a bunch of random ingredients and make a masterpiece meal. God is the Master Chef. You may not like all the ingredients in your life, but when you allow God to mix them all together, folding in His grace and love, He then adds His hope and healing. He begins to add some heat, as we go into the oven of a trial, and something amazing happens in the process. Your faith that was flat begins to rise. Bitterness is overtaken by the sweet. And if you stay in the oven until He says you're finished, people will be lined up just so they can hear the story of what God has done in your life. Every season is a seasoning in God's great recipe.

You may not like all the ingredients in your life, but when you allow God to mix them all together, folding in His grace and love, He then adds His hope and healing.

No wonder Paul, who'd been berated, beaten, imprisoned, and left for dead because of preaching about Jesus, said, "And we know that God causes *all things* to work together for good to those who love God, to those who are called according to His purpose" (Romans 8:28 NASB, emphasis mine). How can he even say that? Have you read the list of ingredients that went into his life before he wrote these words?

> Five times I received from the Jews the forty lashes minus one. Three times I was beaten with rods, once I was pelted with stones, three times I was shipwrecked, I spent a night and a day in the open sea.... I have labored and toiled and have often gone without sleep; I have known hunger and thirst and have often gone without food; I have been cold and naked. (2 Corinthians 11:24–25, 27)

How was Paul able to have all these awful sufferings happen to him and still be able to praise Jesus? Don't you want to know his secret for never quitting in the dip? We can find it in the first verse above from Romans: "And we know..." Right there we hear Paul sharing the secret of the dip. It's *knowing*. We must know that God is in control and that He is working out even the most difficult situations for good, converting even the toughest situation into great benefits. He takes the good, the bad, and the ugly and works them together for the good of those who love Him and who are called according to His purpose.

God doesn't cause all things, but He can work good out of all things. All things. Even when we caused those "things" ourselves. What I mean by that is, because God has given us free will, we can sometimes choose our way into or out of negative circumstances. We live in a broken world where broken people do broken things. But even in your pain, whether caused by you or someone else, God can still use all the circumstances of your dip and work them out for your good. What you're going through right now and what you've been through don't have to be the end.

When you have this mind-set, you're able to see clearer in the storm. You're able to have peace in the turmoil and joy in the middle of the night. Paul sure did. After all that he went through, he wrote, "For our light affliction, which is but for a moment, is working for us a far more exceeding and eternal weight of glory" (2 Corinthians 4:17 NKJV).

This makes me laugh, when you get to this verse and he calls all the dips he's experienced "light affliction." That's not a light affliction. Light affliction is waking up in the middle of the night with a charley horse in your calf and it being sore that day. Paul calls whippings, shipwrecks, beatings, and imprisonments *light affliction*! That's not light. That's massive. That's overwhelming.

The truth is these things were not light or enjoyable on their own. But Paul knew God was working to take all of these ingredients, mix them together, and produce something for His glory. Something that would impact billions of lives for eternity. He would lead jailers to the Lord. He wrote much of the Bible from a jail cell to encourage us today. God used it all.

I'm not making light of what you're going through in the dip. I'm just encouraging you to compare the ingredients of your present situation to what's coming. Your perspective will change once you are standing in your victory looking back at the journey. Where what seemed so heavy then will be light and momentary compared to what's coming.

Paul's words offer a new perspective to the kinds of tests we spoke about in the last chapter. Can we agree that while we're in the test, nothing about it seems light? And it seems to drag on forever. But from God's perspective, He sees the beginning and the end. It's light because God's will for you far outweighs any test you go through. So, once you know this, you can say with confidence, "Bring the heat!" because you know it's only going to help assist you in becoming all God has intended. I know this is difficult to believe when you are smack-dab in the middle of a trial, but if you would take a moment to remember a time in your past when you struggled in a dip that you have now overcome, you can see how you grew and how God worked it out for your good. We don't typically grow on the mountaintop, in the times of ease. We grow in the valley. We grow from resistance. God is the same yesterday, today, and forever. If He brought you out then, He will bring you out now!

SIFTED SAINTS

We've spoken about Simon Peter already, and the little chat Jesus had with him right before He went to the cross. Jesus said to him, "Simon, Simon! Indeed, Satan has asked for you, that he may sift you as wheat. But I have prayed for you, that your faith should not fail; and when you have returned to Me, strengthen your brethren" (Luke 22:31–32 NKJV).

Right here is an example of how a test can prepare someone—and it's a huge one. If tests are the essential ingredients used to produce a great example, this one is a bitter ingredient. Simon Peter is going through a pressurized test where the devil himself is asking to take Peter out. By itself, this test seemed like an unnecessary ingredient. But the devil was asking for Peter. Literally, Jesus was saying, "The devil is begging Me for you." The devil wanted to destroy Peter. Why? Because he must have seen something in Peter that was a threat, so God used it.

Jesus didn't say He would stop the test but He would be with him through the test. Peter would've been very familiar with David's famous words: "Even though I walk *through* the darkest valley, I will fear no evil, for You are with me" (Psalm 23:4, emphasis mine). Allow me to firmly remind you, you're not staying in the valley. You're walking *through* the valley. Don't build a house in the valley. Only pitch a tent in the valley because you're not staying there. You're not staying in the dip. You're walking through.

Jesus said, "I'm here and I'm praying for you." Have you ever had someone tell you they were praying for you and you weren't sure they were? When Jesus tells you, you can rest assured He is. And then Jesus said, "Your faith will falter, but it will not fail." What a gracious Savior we have. Even before Peter could possibly understand what His words meant, Jesus was already planting seeds of hope that Peter would be renewed and restored. When Peter's faith had faltered and he had given up, returning to a life of fishing, that wasn't the end of his story. Jesus showed up with a beachfront breakfast and restored his calling *and* his faith. Jesus' words of prophecy—"and when you have returned to Me, strengthen your brethren" (Luke 22:32)—came true with a vengeance. It was Peter who stepped up and boldly proclaimed the risen Christ on the day of Pentecost, resulting in thousands of people getting saved. It was Peter who led the first megachurch throughout Jerusalem. It was Peter who walked so powerfully in the Holy Spirit that people would get miraculously healed simply by being in the path of his shadow and who wrote books in the Bible. Satan tried to sift Peter as wheat, but God used Peter's test to produce a beautiful loaf of bread that would feed countless people.

Maybe you can again relate to Peter: your life feels like it's facing an all-out attack on your faith. Well, maybe the devil sees you as a threat. Take courage, because Jesus is praying for you (Hebrews 7:25). You can make it through. If you will trust in His strength working within you, you will *always* make it through.

Maybe you're looking back at a test you didn't pass, just as Peter did when he went back to fishing. When you look back at the history of your life and all you see is failure, I want to encourage you that your failure does not have to be final. Your mistakes do not have to define you. Sometimes when we fail, we feel like we're now stuck forever in the dip of our failure. Not true with Jesus! God can turn it around for good. He can forgive and use it to build character, endurance, and strength. Let Peter be your example. Come back to Him. Restore your faith in Jesus so He can restore you, and in turn, you can strengthen others.

There are people who need to hear your story. They need hope to know you made it through. God can use it. He's the Great Recycler;

nothing is wasted with Him. But let Him love and guide you through it because He's got a greater plan that you can't even see right now in the dip.

STAY IN THE OVEN UNTIL THE TIMER GOES OFF

Nobody wants to eat a cake that has only been in the oven for a few minutes. In God's perfect timing, He is making something great out of your circumstances. We have to embrace both the heat of the process and the timing. Things don't always happen overnight, and some processes take longer than others. But just as the individual ingredients meant to create a cake aren't enjoyable to eat on their own, neither is eating a partially baked mess. If you don't embrace the process, you won't achieve the sweet blend of life experiences and tests that are making you grow and preparing you for the next step in your destiny.

I know that embracing God's process is sometimes very difficult. It's hard to wait, especially when your "cake" is starting to smell good and you just want to enjoy it. But you want what's best, not what's okay or good enough. Sometimes in your weariness of enduring you keep asking, "When will it be done?" I'll tell you the answer to that question: when the timer goes off. Trust that God has a will, but He also has a timing. He knows the perfect moment of completion.

With that said, *sometimes* the duration of the test is up to you. Meaning, God sometimes leaves you in longer because there are lessons you are not allowing Him to teach you, things that you must learn in the dip in order to step out of that dip. If you don't, then you'll find yourself repeating the lesson over and over again. For instance, in school there were people who flunked and had to repeat the grade. But then there were a select few who actually learned the lessons so quickly that they skipped a grade and graduated early. Could it be that God is not just interested in the length of the dip, as some sort of punishment or penance, but rather

He's more interested in the lessons learned and the character developed in that dip? Could it be that you could possibly graduate out of the dip earlier than you thought if you learn the lessons more quickly?

Trust God and His timing. He knows what He's doing. To be honest, there have been times when I've not been so sure that He knew what He was doing, but when I've looked back, you know what? I was wrong and He was right. His ways are perfect, and He is always good and faithful. Stay in love with Him, because He promises that all things work together for the good of "those who love Him."

Contrary to popular belief, things don't just have a way of working out on their own in the end. People don't all just get out of dips. I know well-meaning people try to encourage you by saying, "Don't worry. Things have a way of working out in the end." But that's just not true. For some people things end up horribly wrong. It's *God* who works things out. It's *God* who can work good out of the mess. And this is done for those who put Him first. Those who love Him. Let hard times push you *to* God, not away from Him. Be patient and let Him do a complete work in you.

It's *God* who can work good out of the mess. And this is done for those who put Him first. Those who love Him.

As you are embracing the process, remember this verse: "Cast your cares on the LORD and he will sustain you; he will never let the righteous be shaken" (Psalm 55:22). I love this verse! You think you can't make it through the test? Let me encourage you with a great picture of this verse. A while back I was on a plane that had just landed. Don't you hate it when the plane has barely touched ground and everybody is already standing up waiting to disembark? No one is moving, and you're stuck there. Everyone crowds the aisle and we all just look at each other.

On this particular flight, we were all doing just that. But there was a boy who couldn't have been more than five years old. He was wearing a backpack, and in frustration with this burden on his back he began to cry, then looked at his mom and said, "Mom! It's too heavy!" His mother's response was to reach two fingers down and loop them under the little strap on top of the backpack. She then lifted it up just an inch or so and said, "How's that?" The little guy stopped crying, sniffed, and said, "That's better, Mom." The weight of the backpack didn't change. The distribution of the weight changed, which made it manageable. When you cast your cares on the Lord, the weight of your burden doesn't change. The distribution of the weight changes where you shift the weight to God. That's a great picture of this verse!

You were never meant to carry your burdens alone. They're too heavy. By saying this, I'm not talking about how I hear Christians sometimes trying to encourage each other by saying, "Don't worry, you know what the Bible says: 'God won't give you more than you can bear.'" Because that's just NOT TRUE! That's not in the Bible. I've checked. They're misquoting 1 Corinthians 10:13, which says that God "will not let you to be *tempted* beyond what you can bear. But when you are tempted, he will also provide a way out so that you can endure it" (emphasis mine).

I think we can all raise our hands and say we have all had more than we can bear. We have all had more than we can handle. That's why we have verses like Psalm 55:22. When a burden comes, we're not to try and carry it all on our own. When a test comes, we're not made to stay in the hot oven of testing on our own. We're to embrace the process by giving our burden to God and allowing *Him* to do the perfect work inside of us. He's the one who reaches down and supernaturally undergirds us and sustains us in ways that we never thought were possible.

Embrace the process. He's working all the ingredients of your life together for good when you love Him and put Him first. Trust Him. And then allow Him to use all that He has produced in you to help and encourage others. You're coming back!

Chapter 14

SUPERSET

My favorite part of working out is when I get to rest. I'm a huge fan of the Pilates child's pose, where I get to lie down on the mat. The room where this takes place is waaaay better than the weight room I described earlier with all the grunting and posturing. In the Pilates room there is soft music playing and nice squishy mats. And when you get done with the workout, the instructor hands out lavender-infused warm towels to wipe your face. Or so I've heard. From a friend.

There are so many different ways to work out at the gym. Pilates, aerobics, cycling, free weights. I inevitably end up in the room with all the grunting, ready to "get swole" by lifting as much weight as I possibly can. Normally, when you use free weights, you do what's called a set. That's when you lift a certain weight a certain number of times, and then you rest for a minute or so. No child's pose in the weight room, though, unless you want to get punched. The short rest in between sets is important because it gives your muscles a chance to recuperate.

During a season when I was using a trainer, he taught me about a different kind of workout called a "superset." This is where you do one activity or weight lift, then quickly move on to another one, and then—you guessed it—a third one. You do all this without any rest. I know! That squishy mat and lavender-infused face towel were looking better by the minute.

So as I was struggling through two to three heavy activities back-to-back, with no rest, the obvious question I asked the trainer was, "Why are you torturing me like this?" He explained that when you move from strength exercise to strength exercise with no resting in between, it causes your muscles to work harder, and you can get better results faster. The superset doesn't feel good, but later on it feels great to see the results.

I hope you're seeing this. There are seasons where you have a test and then rest. Test, then rest. But I feel there are other seasons when it seems as if God allows you to go through a superset of tests. It's test, then test, then test. Some of you in the dip feel that way right now. You've been going from one test to another. One wave after another. And you're wondering why. Could it be that He's getting you ready faster? Perhaps He wants you to be ready for a particular aspect of your calling and there is an expedited path that requires you to be developed quicker. Sometimes that means more tests. But don't let that discourage you! Remember, He's always with you. You're never alone.

Think about this. Isn't it funny how people will pay a trainer because they want to see results and yet for the entirety of the workout they complain to the trainer, "I can't do this. It's too much. You're trying to kill me." How do you expect to get *there* if you don't embrace the development *here*? We desire growth and yet reject what grows us. How do you expect to get the results you desire if you don't embrace the stretching? You stretch to reach further. Supersets are not fun in the middle of the workout, but just as we discussed in the previous chapter, once we've embraced the process, the result God brings out is always good!

REFRESHMENT

Here's a key to making it through the superset—or any kind of set, for that matter—alive. For many years when I worked out at the gym, I would not carry around a water bottle. One day after I had finished my workout with a trip into the sauna, there was an older gentleman who was already in there. I sat down and looked forward, as every guy does when he's in close quarters with another guy in the sauna. It was dead quiet. Then, out of nowhere, breaking the silence, that guy speaks up in a loud, authoritative, booming voice. "Where's your water?" I about jumped out of my seat. "Excuse me?" I asked, trying to figure out exactly why this stranger was speaking to me in such a harsh tone. He repeated, "Where's your water?" I have to admit I was a little irritated and thought he should just mind his own business.

Once we've embraced the process, the result God brings out is always good!

Without any prompting from me, he proceeded, "I was an EMT for thirty years, and what I've observed is that most people are dehydrated before they ever even step in here."

Guess what? I bring a water bottle to the gym now. Ha! But here's what I found out. Since I had not yet developed the habit of carrying the water bottle with me, I'd set it down at a machine, work out, and then move to the next machine, leaving my water bottle behind. In other words, I would go from one test to another while leaving my refreshment behind.

Here's what I felt God say to me about spiritual health one day: Some of us have not yet developed the habit of taking our refreshment with us. We go from one test to another. The test is not the problem. Refreshment is. Some of us are so dehydrated spiritually, but we think we can pass the test without refreshment. God is our refreshment! That's why the psalmist writes, "As the deer longs for streams of water, so I long for you, O God. I thirst for God, the living God. When can I go and stand before him?" (Psalm 42:1–2 NLT).

David went through test after test in order to prepare to be the greatest king in the nation. And as much as life would leave him dry and thirsty, he knew, "The LORD is my shepherd, I lack nothing. He makes me lie down in green pastures, he leads me beside quiet waters, he refreshes my soul" (Psalm 23:1–3). Listen. Stay close to the source, because a test with refreshment can strengthen you. A test without refreshment, though, can kill you.

When we are tired and worn out from the dip we are in, we need to remember what Jesus said to the woman at the well: "Everyone who drinks this water will be thirsty again, but whoever drinks the water I give them will never thirst. Indeed, the water I give them will become in them a spring of water welling up to eternal life" (John 4:13–14). We need these springs of living water bubbling up from inside us at all times.

Jesus is the Living Water. Only He can refresh and satisfy. Jeremiah 31:25 promises us that God "will refresh the weary and satisfy the faint." Maybe no one else knows how tired you really are, but God knows, and He sees you. He wants to give you a refreshed soul, restored strength, and a joy-filled life.

You won't find true refreshment any other place. No amount of money can refresh your soul. There are plenty of people with more money than they could possibly spend in a lifetime, and they still hate themselves. You won't find refreshment in a bottle of pills or a bottle of alcohol. You won't find it in popularity or a relationship. Jesus is the Living Water that you need.

Think about the hottest day you've ever experienced. Picture me walking up to you on that day, when you're so thirsty, and I offer you a cup of lukewarm milk. No way! Your body needs water. Even though we often reach for other beverages, our body craves water. There's nothing like ice-cold water on a scorching-hot day. I know we reach for all sorts of things when we have a thirsty soul, but what our soul is really craving is Jesus.

IN TRAINING

You've heard the saying "No pain, no gain." When working out, you need to get uncomfortable to see results. Comfort cannot be your priority. We love comfort. Comfortable beds. Comfortable shoes. Comfortable conversations with comfortable people. Comfortable schedules. I love comfort too, but I don't think God wants you so comfortable that you don't follow Him into your destiny. That's not a win. That's a letdown. God is more concerned with your character and calling than your comfort. "Not only so, but we also glory in our sufferings, because we know that suffering produces perseverance; perseverance, character; and character, hope" (Romans 5:3–4). If we start with the end result, we find that if we want hope, that comes with character. But if we want character, that comes from perseverance. And the only way to get perseverance is by going through some stuff.

Professional football players aren't comfortable at training camp or toward the end of a hard-fought game. That's difficult and grueling work. But they also get the privilege of making history by playing in the NFL. And some even get to play in the Super Bowl. A select few receive a ring because they win the Super Bowl. You know who's comfortable during football season? The guy at home in his La-Z-Boy recliner, eating a bowl of chips while watching other people live out their dreams.

I don't want you to just watch other people live out their dreams; I want you to live out your own God dreams. Don't make comfort your main priority; make obeying God your priority. The number one goal needs to be development and health. The same goes for you spiritually when you are in the dip. Trust that God is working in you, building you up, making you stronger. Let Him finish. God is training you, so decide today that you will stay trainable. In 2 Timothy 3:16–17, it says, "All Scripture is God-breathed and is useful for teaching, rebuking, correcting and training in righteousness, so that the servant of God may be thoroughly equipped for every good work."

Did you see *how* God trains? With His Word, and sometimes teaching. Sometimes rebuking. That doesn't sound fun. Correcting? I thought God was just about sunshine and butterflies. Shaun, are you telling me there will be times when He rebukes and corrects? Yes. Why? Because He is training you. That's what trainers do. They model, encourage, and correct. Training must take place if you're going to be equipped.

When you work out, you tear down muscle, then let it heal and grow, and repeat that process over and over. Maybe for you there's been a tearing, but you haven't allowed God to heal you. You've been going through a test and instead of seeing growth, you're just experiencing more pain. More pain, but no gain. If this is you, I invite you to stop for a second right now and invite God to heal you so you can be restored. Ask Him what kind of specific refreshment you need to properly heal in this season. Make sure to carve out extra time, simply to sit in His presence and allow Him to be your Good Shepherd, who allows you to lie down so that He can restore your soul.

SPOT ME, BRO!

In the gym, when someone is lifting a lot of weight, he'll ask another person to spot him. To spot someone means you stand by him, watching him lift the weights. If he happens to get stuck, and the weight is too heavy to complete the lift, the spotter steps in and helps him lift what he could not lift on his own.

Ecclesiastes 4:9–10 describes this spiritual truth: "Two are better than one, because they have a good return for their labor: If either of them falls down, one can help the other up. But pity anyone who falls and has no one to help them up."

The point is clear. If you're all alone when you fall in life—into depression, sin, or anger—you're in trouble. If you fall with a friend, they can help lift you back up right away. Friends won't let you stay there. They'll pray with you. They'll reach out to help you and to encourage you to be who God has called you to be. It's hard to quit in the dip when you've got friends eager to pull you out of it. By yourself you're open to attack.

If you want to be healed from your yesterdays, God has a formula: "Confess your sins to each other and pray for each other so that you may be *healed*" (James 5:16, emphasis mine). We confess to God to receive forgiveness (1 John 1:9). But God set it up for us to receive healing by going to one another. But you won't go to someone else unless you can trust them. And you can't trust them without relationship. So that's why having a small group of people who are spiritually like-minded and are going the same way as you is so important. You need people in your life who can help spot you when the test gets too heavy. People to help lift. People to help encourage and pray for you. To talk with. A few trusted people that you can let know what you're struggling with. When I work out with a spotter and I want to quit, he's right there cheering me on. "You can do three more! Come on! Two more! You've got this! One more!" My spotter pushes me beyond what I think I can do on my own, and he's there in case the weight gets to be too much.

You definitely need a spotter, but you also need to *be* a spotter for someone else. Don't just think people should spot you. Who can you be a spotter for, and how can you help them? None of us ever arrives where God wants us to be on our own. We need each other, always praying for, teaching, correcting, loving, encouraging, and helping one another. Ephesians 4:16 says, "From [Jesus] the whole body, joined and held together by every supporting ligament, grows and builds itself up in love, as each part does its work."

The *body* is the church, and our job is to build one another up. A lot of bodybuilders spend so much time building muscle to go on a competitive stage and flex. That's awesome. But I'm thinking, *Come over here and let's put those muscles to work. Help me move this couch. Lift this mirror. Do something.* In other words: The development is not just for you to go onstage and be in the spotlight. God is building you to build others. He's maturing you in order for you to be in a place to offer wisdom to others. Let's not just admire how spiritually developed we are. Let's be on the lookout to see where we can use our muscles to help lift and build people up.

God is building you to build others. He's maturing you in order for you to be in a place to offer wisdom to others.

INTERLOCKED

There are redwood trees in the San Francisco area. They're massive. Sturdy. And ridiculously strong. But not just because of their height or depth or width. There's something fascinating about these trees. Their roots grow down deep, but there's more to it than that. Their roots grow down and interlock with other roots from other redwood trees, making them incredibly strong. When the winds and the storms come, they're immovable and unshakable. It's time to get planted in a church and let your roots go down deep and invite others into your life to help spot you.

In the same way, your life will be so much stronger when you let your roots go down deep and interlock with other believers going the same way as you. Plant yourself in the House of the Lord, in a good Bible-believing church.

Psalm 92:13 teaches us that "[he who is] planted in the House of the Lord...will flourish in the courts of our God."

We all want to flourish, but we don't want to be planted. Think about the old Western movies. There was always a gunfight on a dusty road, as two people stood facing each other. Then, cue the music. Can you hear the whistle and the guitar? Inevitably, there was always a tumbleweed that would blow by. Why are tumbleweeds always blowing down the street? The answer is easy. They're really big on top but they have itty-bitty roots. You never see a redwood tree blowing down the road in those movies. They're too strong. When the winds and storms come, they're immovable. As believers, let's be redwoods and not tumbleweeds.

One last thing my trainer taught me was that while trying to get in shape through those amazing supersets, what I did outside the gym was just as important. My diet was crucial to seeing results from the supersets. Yet another strong spiritual truth! I wonder if my trainer has ever considered becoming a preacher. As we go through the dip, we really need to watch what we are ingesting. We have to guard what we are allowing into our minds. Typically, people don't give much thought to their spiritual intake. Any TV show. Any music artist. Any movie. Any advice. Any thought. Any podcast. We ingest so much junk and then wonder why we don't feel good. It's like pigging out at the buffet every night...and then picking up a dozen donuts on your way home. You're working out but not seeing the results you desire because the diet is unhealthy. You'll be miserable because of all the junk you're taking in.

Set some guardrails up for what you will and will not allow into your heart. Get into a good Bible-believing church. Join a small group of people going the same way as you. Open up the Bible and begin to read.

Discover who Jesus is, and when you do, you'll begin to see who you are in Him. Remember, God's plan includes you finishing well. He has started something in your life, so let Him carry it to completion. Determine that you're going to be committed to the workout, committed to guarding your intake, committed to finding a spotter and becoming a spotter, and you watch, as you embrace the process, and by not quitting in the dip, you will grow so much that in a few years, you won't be able to recognize the spiritual giant you've become!

Chapter 15

TURNING TO GOD

Driving through San Francisco, you notice that the streets are so narrow and steep *and* overpopulated that you feel like you're on a roller coaster. It's not for the faint of heart, let me tell you. One night years ago, in the prehistoric age before GPS—I'm talking about back during the 1900s—my wife and I were braving the San Fran city streets, once again on the hunt for a good restaurant. I turned left and a guy on the street started screaming at me for no reason. "Hey! Hey you!" His arms were flailing all around, and he seemed out of his mind. I looked at my wife and said, "Don't look to the right; there's a crazy person." It's not unusual to have a random stranger yell at you in San Francisco. I cupped my hand and brought it up to hide my face, breathing a sigh of relief when I was almost past him, but this dude was unrelenting. "Hey! You! Turn around now! You! Turn around!"

All of a sudden, his mania made sense. I was on a one-way street… going the wrong way! Screeching to a halt on this narrow street, I flipped the car in reverse and made the quickest seventeen-point turn you've ever seen in your life. Drove forward. Turned hard left. Put it in reverse. Steered hard right. Over and over as fast as I could. Several large trucks and cars were coming right at us, with their drivers honking their horns and using hand gestures to tell us we were number one, if you know what I mean. Finally, we were facing the correct direction and were saved.

Let me tell you, my whole view of that man changed. This time, when I drove back by him, he was no longer a crazy person; he was my best friend. I rolled my window down, gave him a thumbs-up, and said, "Thanks, buddy! Keep America safe!"

Isn't it funny how we can view people the wrong way, based on our perception? Sometimes we find ourselves in a dip because we drove the wrong way and crashed into that dip with a bad decision. That's a horrible feeling, wondering if God will even allow a U-turn. Maybe you're wondering if you can turn around. Of course you can! You can totally turn around. As a matter of fact, if you find yourself going the wrong way in life, I'm urging you to turn around.

The Bible has a word for turning around: *repent*. When you read that word, please don't look at me as if I'm some crazy person, yelling at you from the side of the street, "Hey! You! Turn around! Yeah, you! Turn around now!" Like my newfound friend in San Francisco, I'm just trying to keep you from crashing!

It's not just about believing in Jesus; it's about obeying Him and following His directions for your life.

To repent simply means to turn around. You are going your way, and then you turn around and start going God's way. You change direction. This might be the very key to getting out of the dip. It's not just about believing in Jesus; it's about obeying Him and following His directions for your life.

HELP TO REACH THE NEXT LEVEL

Let me say it another way: it's submitting the control of your life to Him. When I was young, I played on my Nintendo a lot. Remember, I'm talking about the original Nintendo. One summer day, I was playing *Super Mario Bros.*, and I just couldn't conquer this one level. Every time I would try, I'd die. And then that music would play, that death song. I can hear it in my head now. A friend who was hanging out with me that day watched me die over and over before he became very frustrated. He was great at this game and offered, "Shaun, give me the controller. I'll pass the level for you." To which I said, "No! I've got it. I want to do it myself." But then I just repeated the process of getting stumped then dying, and having to hear the death song again. I did this an embarrassing number of times. Finally, after coming to the painstaking realization that I couldn't do this on my own, I begrudgingly gave my friend the controller, and just like he said, he conquered the level for me.

Does this sound familiar? Do you know what it's like to be stuck in the dip and you keep trying to get out by yourself? You keep trying to pass the test or the level, but every time you keep crashing. You keep making the wrong decisions. Keep clicking. Keep stumbling. Keep failing. It's so disheartening to feel like you can do it on your own and then having to admit that no matter how hard you try, you just keep ending back at the same spot: smack-dab in the middle of the dip.

We think, *I've got this. I can do this on my own.* The world around us tells us we can. But the truth is we don't "got this." We can't do this on our own. We've been stuck, on the same level, for way too long now, trapped in the dip. Why don't you give the controller to God? He's already conquered all the levels. He knows where all the secret passageways are, and He's asking you, "Give the control of your life over to Me." Stop trying to dig your way out of the dip yourself.

It takes faith to do this. It takes admitting we can't do everything in our own strength. We have placed our trust in so many other things, and it hasn't worked. If it had, you wouldn't be reading this book. I'm about to become your best friend right now. I want to encourage you to put all your faith, trust, and dependence on Jesus. Going your own way, apart from Jesus, always leads to death. Spiritual death. Death to a relationship. Death to a dream. A destiny. But remember, Jesus is the One who has abundant life ready and waiting for you, but you've got to give Him the control of your life. It's called surrender. And when you surrender fully to Him, you'll watch as God comes in and floods your soul with so much grace.

CAN I TURN?

You might be reading this and thinking, *I can't turn to God.* Maybe you feel you've done too much or gone too far. Not true. You read Acts 3:19, "Repent, then, and turn to God," and you immediately break out in a sweat. This is great news. Look at the next part: "so that your sins may be wiped out, that times of refreshing may come from the Lord." What a verse! When you repent, He's not waiting to punish you; He wants to wipe your sins out. Completely! But wait. There's more! If you call right now…He'll send a time of refreshing to your soul. Refreshment doesn't come without having our sins wiped out. And our sins don't get wiped out without turning to God in repentance. But we won't turn to God unless we see Him the right way. He wants you to see Him as your loving heavenly Father. "God's kindness is intended to lead you to repentance" (Romans 2:4). Let me share with you one of the most famous stories from the Bible to demonstrate how extraordinary and lavish God's love for us is.

Jesus expressed this story in Luke 15 to communicate His heart for us when we've strayed. A father had two sons. One son asked for his share of the inheritance so he could leave home to pursue his own pleasures. You have to understand, in this culture, asking for his inheritance before his father passed would've been like slapping his father in the face and saying, "I wish you were dead. Give me my money now!"

The father granted his request and the young man took off, thinking he was going to have the time of his life. He had a time all right. He did whatever his little heart desired. He went to his Las Vegas equivalent, indulged in all the wild parties and women, lived it up, until all his money was gone. Funny, when his money was gone, so were his friends. He eventually found himself feeding pigs just to barely get by, which in his culture would've been unheard of since pigs were considered unclean and untouchable. But he was so desperate he felt he had run out of options. The Bible records that he was so hungry he longed to fill his stomach with the pig slop. That's desperate. I might look at the pigs and want to eat them, but pig slop? He was in a big ol' dirty dip.

He finally had a thought that he had probably fought off for a while. He rationalized, "The people who work for my father are living better than I am right now. I know I can't go back to being a son, I've failed that miserably, but maybe my father will allow me to just work for him." He started his journey back home.

I want you to put yourself in his place right now, because really, he is us in the story. He's nervous. He's apprehensive. Full of shame for how he'd failed, he hit such a low point that he finally realized, *I am out of control and I need help.* He was sure his father would shun him for his poor decisions. He probably expected the biggest lecture with many *I told you so*'s. So he braced himself for the judgment that he knew he deserved.

But to his shock and utter amazement, when the son returned home, his father was waiting for him. When the father saw his son returning, he ran to him. Again, understanding the culture, dignified men did not run anywhere. But the father didn't care about his dignity; he cared about his son.

The son tried to recite the speech he had rehearsed on his three-by-five cards, but his father didn't even let him finish. He grabbed his son, hugged him, kissed him, and yelled to his staff, "Put a robe on my son, put sandals on his feet and a ring on his finger! And kill the fatted calf because we're having filet mignon tonight! My son who was lost is found. My son who I thought was dead is alive!" They threw the biggest party to celebrate his son's return and the father restored the son to his original place of honor. Can you imagine how dizzy this young man would've been by overwhelming grace? He would have found this unexpected reception unbelievable.

I know you're a little hesitant when you think about what kind of reception you'd get from God. I mean, after all, we have all gone our own way. We're embarrassed, we're confused, and as much as we know we need God, we're just a bit uncertain as to how or *if* He'll receive us.

I was at the Sacramento airport, having just come home from a trip. I descended the escalator into the baggage claim area and approached the carousel to retrieve my luggage, and then waited for my ride. And waited. And waited some more. Finally, I called our office to find out how much longer I had to wait for a ride, and they informed me that our assistant had forgotten to schedule a pickup for me. My ride was an hour and a half away.

What else is there to do at an airport but watch people? Sitting on a bench near the escalator, I noticed all the people waiting to greet their friends and family. Some had flowers, others had signs. I watched as a girlfriend was greeted by her boyfriend. I saw a mom and her kids welcome their grandparents. Each reunion was heartfelt and very touching.

But then I saw this grown man, who had to be about fifty. He was huge. Incredibly buff. He had an intense scowl on his face, as if he wanted to fight somebody. As he paced back and forth, noticeably agitated, I thought, *What's wrong with this guy?* And then it all made sense when a young man in army fatigues came down the escalator and locked eyes with the man. It was this man's son coming back from war. You should have seen this. The huge, burly dad ran to the son. The son ran to the dad. And their bodies slammed into the strongest, biggest hug I have ever witnessed in my entire life. They were holding each other, both crying uncontrollably. It was so intense, with so much emotion. They didn't care who else was around in this crowded airport. It was the greatest reunion I've ever seen. And all I could think was, *Man, no one came to greet me. Maybe I can get in on a group hug.* I'm kidding.

I'll never forget what I saw that day. It's burned in my memory, and it is exactly how I picture the father greeting his prodigal son. And this is what you need to think about when you're contemplating coming back to Jesus. Whatever other picture you have in your mind, thinking He won't accept you is not right. Even a picture of God just kind of casually nodding His head at your return is not right either.

I need you to understand that your view of God will determine your approach to God. Jesus gave us this story in Luke 15 for a reason, to help us when we're insecure about how He'll receive us. He said this is how: watch as the father, after seeking every night for his long-lost son, pulled up his robe and sprinted to embrace him. You need to see Him like that father at the airport. Running to you. Embracing you. So filled with joy to have you home.

> Your view of God will determine your approach to God.

This is the story of the prodigal son. Most of the time we refer to the prodigal son as the lost son. And that he was. But the definition of *prodigal* does not mean lost. It means wasteful. It means to squander. When we waste what we are given by God, we push ourselves away from God, losing our sense of purpose, meaning, and direction. This is how we get lost and wind up in a dip thinking we can never come home. Well, reading this chapter today, you now know this isn't true. There's still hope and healing in the dip, even when you feel lost. Come home.

This is not really a story about the son; it is a story about the love of the Father. How our heavenly Father responds to lost children coming back to Him. See God this way. And maybe you haven't yet surrendered the control of your life to Jesus, as we talked about previously. Or maybe you were once close but have drifted away. Maybe you're not as close to God as you once were, or maybe there's an area of your life that you haven't totally surrendered, or maybe there's something from your past. Could it be your family? Your finances? A relationship? Anxiety? Whatever it is, I'd love to lead you in a commitment prayer. It would be my honor to lead you back to Jesus and watch Him flood your life with grace and forgiveness.

As you read this, make these words your own:

> *Lord Jesus, thank You for loving me right where I am. Today, I'm coming home. Please forgive all of my sins. Wash me clean. I place my trust in You alone for salvation, and I surrender the control of my life to You. Be my Lord and Savior. From this day forward, I'm all Yours. I love You. In Jesus' name I pray, amen.*

SECTION FIVE

Chapter 16

BYE, BYE, FEAR

It's 1989. The year Bobby Brown and Paula Abdul had the top trending songs. The year the Oakland A's won the World Series and the 49ers won the Super Bowl. When *Back to the Future Part II* and *Honey, I Shrunk the Kids* were the leading blockbuster movies. But there was about to be an even bigger story that year: my very first roller-coaster ride.

Some friends and I, along with my older brother, Chad, decided to go to a theme park in the Bay Area called Great America. At eleven years of age, I was terrified of roller coasters. Summer after summer, my friends would try coercing me to hop into one of these death traps, but I would avoid the issue by overcompensating with the "spinny rides." I pretended to love these rides, but let's be honest: nobody loves the spinny rides. They make you vomit. But I had to go on something so I could conveniently not have time to risk my life on the roller coasters. So my life was relegated to me saying, "Hey, guys, you should really try these teacups! They're crazy!" Sad, right? I know.

But on this fateful day in 1989, they weren't buying it. The moment we entered the park, overshadowed by the monstrous coasters, my friend started pressing me to ride one of the biggest, scariest roller coasters in the park. "Come on, Shaun. Let's go!" As soon as those terrifying words came out of his mouth, it was like I went deaf for a minute. Everything was moving in slow motion, like in those war movies when a grenade goes off. My eyes glossed over. And then I heard one faint voice in the background whisper, "He won't go; he's too scared." My older brother of seven years came to my defense and said, "Don't worry. I'll go with you."

Somehow I found myself in line, where the real torment began. For an hour, I had to snake back and forth beneath that massive roller coaster. For that entire hour, everyone was laughing and joking to pass the time, but all I could focus on was the roller coaster whizzing overtop and the bloodcurdling screams of terror raining down. We turned the final corner and I could see the end of the line. The end of my life! Everyone else was completely unfazed by this torture machine, smiling and joking around while my heart was pounding out of my chest. Frozen in time, there came a gap in the line ahead of me and the people behind me were yelling, "Move up, buddy!"

At this point, I did what any sane person would do in this predicament. I tried to get out of it. Stuttering, trying to come up with a good excuse, I said sheepishly, "Hey, guys, I'm just going to wait for you at the exit. I'm...I'm thirsty. I...I really need a drink. I have to go to the bathroom." My friend attempted to help by saying, "Shaun, look at that little girl that just got off the ride. She's like six years old. If she can do it, you can do it." Well, that didn't motivate me. Now I was afraid *and* ashamed.

It was time. We were next. The car pulled up and I had every intention of stepping into it and stepping right through to the other side so I could run for the exit, but my brother grabbed me and lowered that bar that locks you in place. Now I couldn't move. I couldn't breathe.

Couldn't swallow. "You've got to get me out. I can't…I can't breathe! Let me out!" But it was too late. The worker mocked me over the loudspeaker with her terrifying voice: "Enjoy your ride at Great America." Oh, and by the way, it didn't help that the roller coaster was named the Demon! I knew this was my day to die.

The train slowly clicked off. We entered into a dark tunnel that was quickly filled with screams. The puppylike whimpers may or may not have been mine. We began climbing with that terrifying *clink*, *clink*, *clink*, each sounding off another few feet of our ascent. To say I was frightened would be the biggest understatement. I was horrified. Right then and there, in sheer desperation, I reached over and grabbed my older brother's hand. We were holding hands, INTERLOCKING FINGERS! This was it. No turning back as the car reached the summit. And then came the dip. We free-fell for what seemed a thousand feet. I let out a scream. Not a cool, manly scream. It sounded like an eleven-year-old-girl-at-a-Justin-Bieber-concert scream. We zoomed right into two loop-the-loops and three corkscrews. It was fast. It was scary. But when that train came to a halt, the adrenaline kicked in and I heard myself shout, "Let's do it again!" I conquered that Demon, in Jesus' name, and now I love roller coasters.

AFRAID

There's a lot that people are afraid of in life. Terrorism. Heights. Spiders. Confined spaces. Public speaking. Being alone. Fear is the unpleasant, powerful, and often debilitating emotion we feel when we sense or anticipate danger. When we are in a dip, fear is not a faithful friend; it's a ferocious foe. And for some of us, *fear* is the name of the pit we live in. I know. I've been there. I was deep in the dip of fear for a long time, and I couldn't see a way out. As a kid, I worried about everything. I couldn't even be away from home. I'd try sleepovers at friends' houses, but they would always end up the same: me calling my mom to come pick me up. At night, I needed my mom to check on me every few minutes before falling asleep. By second grade, I had developed a stomach ulcer.

You'd think I'd just grow out of it. But you don't grow out of fear. Fear is a spirit. If anything, you just grow older and switch fears. For me it led to panic attacks. Chest pains. Emergency hospital visits. And as I briefly explained in chapter 2, my stomach pains got progressively worse, to the point where I'd be doubled over, on the ground, in the fetal position for hours. There was nothing that could bring relief. Even morphine in the hospital would just barely take the edge off. When I say it dominated my life, I'm saying that it controlled me. It dictated the direction of my life…for my first twenty-five years.

This fear led to extreme vacillation, where I couldn't make a decision. The simplest decision of what shirt to wear would become a thirty-minute ordeal. Standing there, looking at the clothes in my closet, unable to make a decision, I would be sweating and panicking. This might seem ridiculous, but every time I speak about this, people come up to tell me they are currently experiencing the exact same thing. It's unbearable.

WHY DO WE FEAR?

The disciples of Jesus were fighting through a storm. Not just any kind of storm, but one of hurricane-like proportions. These experienced fishermen were completely caught off guard by the ferocity of this storm, and they greatly feared for their lives (Mark 4:35–41). To make matters worse, Jesus was sleeping in the bottom of the boat! I knew naps were spiritual. Jesus was taking a nap. The disciples came running to wake Him up with their screams: "Help! We're going to drown!" Jesus responded, "You of little faith, *why* are you so afraid?"

Chris Hodges helped me see how interesting it is that Jesus never asked them *what* they were afraid of. He asked them *why* they were afraid. For Jesus, the question was not, "Which phobias do you have?" To Him, the answers to that were irrelevant. The real question was, "How can you be afraid when I'm right here with you?" I believe He's asking us the same question today. There were actually three storms going. A physical one: the winds and waves. An emotional storm: their fear. And a spiritual storm: their wrong theology. They thought Jesus didn't care. He got up and calmed all three.

At least the disciples knew who to go to when they were afraid. They ran to Jesus. Can I recommend you do the same? Spending time with someone builds a relationship, and a relationship breeds trust. You wouldn't trust a complete stranger with your phone. You wouldn't hand off your crying baby to a person you just met at the airport. But you'd trust your closest friend. The closer you are to someone, the more you're able to trust them.

Why do we fear? Because we lack confidence in Jesus. We're not sure we're going to be okay. Jesus is calling us into a closer relationship with Him so we can turn our fears into trust. You can trust in Jesus.

There are many verses in the Bible to remind you that peace comes from God. You can live a life of peace when you know God is with you. Here are just a few reminders:

> Have I not commanded you? Be strong and courageous. Do not be afraid; do not be discouraged, for the Lord your God will be with you wherever you go. (Joshua 1:9)

> I sought the Lord, and he answered me; he delivered me from all my fears. (Psalm 34:4)

> Do not be anxious about anything, but in every situation, by prayer and petition, with thanksgiving, present your requests to God. And the peace of God, which transcends all understanding,

> will guard your hearts and your minds in Christ Jesus. (Philippians 4:6–7)

Fear assumes and expects the worst while faith assumes and expects the best. Fear causes you to exaggerate the problem. Remember being at home alone as a kid? You heard one thing and your eyes got big as you stared at a window, waiting to hear another noise. Pretty soon you were convinced someone wearing a hockey mask was hiding in your house.

Panic leads to more panic. Don't feed fear. Don't entertain fear and don't be entertained by fear. Horror movies are a multimillion-dollar industry. People pay money to be entertained by fear! I don't get that. To entertain is to welcome something or someone in, to hold it close to your heart and mind. Life can be scary enough, let alone inviting in and submitting yourself to images that can haunt you for years. You can't unsee that kind of stuff.

Fear can take root in your mind, and if left unchecked, it will only grow. Don't fertilize those roots by entertaining thoughts of fear, or by imagining and meditating on worst-case scenarios. Instead, make a decision to guard your mind and to "take captive every thought to make it obedient to Christ" (2 Corinthians 10:5).

When a thought comes into your mind, ask God, "Lord, is this thought from you or not?" If it's not, throw it out. One of the best ways of getting rid of a thought is to think about something else. Blue! Blue sky. Clouds. Huge, fluffy clouds that look like vanilla cotton candy. See? I just gave you a new thought. And immediately, you started imagining blue skies. Fill your mind with other things and push the wrong thoughts out.

Remembering that fear is a spirit, keep in mind that "God has not given us a spirit of fear, but of power and of love and of a sound mind" (2 Timothy 1:7 NKJV). In addition, Jesus told us, "Peace I leave with you;

my peace I give you. I do not give to you as the world gives. Do not let your hearts be troubled and do not be afraid" (John 14:27).

BREAKING FREE

God is willing and able to deliver you from not some but *all* of your fears. Let me share with you a major key for breaking free of fear. I told you my life was dominated by fear for the first twenty-five years. Well, what I didn't tell you was that my grandmother was a worrier, my dad was a worrier, and one of our daughters, Victoria, became a worrier. Yep. She started down the same road. She cried in fear every night. I'd ask, "What are you afraid of?" and she'd cry out, "I don't know!" That's the crazy thing about fear. Sometimes, you don't even know what it is that you're afraid of. You're just afraid, and this keeps you locked like a prisoner in a dip of intense fear.

This lasted for years. When she was around eight, I looked at the tears of fear streaming down her face one night as I was tucking her in. I said, "I think I passed this down to you. And I'm sorry." Of course, in her little mind, she didn't understand, so she cried out, "Why did you give this to me?!" I said, "No. Not like that. I mean, I used to deal with fear just like this too. But we're going to break it for you the same way I did." We took the verse 1 John 4:18, and we banked on it: "Perfect love drives out fear." Read that again.

If you're struggling with fear, and that verse is true, then you don't need to get more bold. You need to get more love! Because God's perfect love drives out fear. In other words, fear cannot stay where God's love resides. God's love and your fear cannot cohabitate the same space. God's love comes in and serves your fear an eviction notice. Isn't it great that God's love "drives out" fear? It doesn't politely ask fear if it would be okay leaving sometime in the future. No! God's love literally kicks out, drives out, forces out fear. His love overpowers fear. I've heard it said that faith is the opposite of fear. I don't think that's entirely accurate. I don't think faith is the opposite of fear. *Love* is the opposite of fear. And when you open up your heart to the everlasting love of Jesus, His love comes in and pushes fear completely out.

God's love literally kicks out, drives out, forces out fear. His love overpowers fear.

So with Victoria's big, beautiful eyes staring at me, still filled with tears, I said, "We're going to break this. Perfect love drives out fear." And for the next several weeks, every night as she would lie in bed and be tormented by fear, I didn't spend my time rebuking fear. I spent my time singing songs of God's love. Every song I could think about. I'd quote verses of God's love, reinforcing the fact that she was so incredibly loved by God. Accepted by God. That He is crazy in love with her and so are her mom and dad. And I'm so grateful to report that after several weeks of this, that spirit of fear broke, and Victoria is completely free from fear dominating her life!

As a father, it broke my heart to see our daughter going through something she didn't have to go through. I was committed to seeing her set free. In the same way, your heavenly Father doesn't want you going through something you don't have to go through, and He's committed to setting you free.

This is how God broke the reign of fear over my life, over our daughter's life, and I know God doesn't want you to be ruled by fear any longer. God didn't give this to you. So if it's not from Him, then don't accept it. It's like when we receive a package that we didn't order. Just because it was delivered to your house doesn't mean you have to accept it. That's been our problem. The devil has been shipping us things, and just because it lands on our doorstep and has our name printed on the label, we feel obligated to accept it. No way! It's time we say, "Return to sender!" It's time to take that fear and send it back to hell where it belongs. It cannot stay at your house anymore. God loves you. He adores you. And it's time to open up your heart and receive His love. Then watch as fear packs its bags and runs away.

God is love. The world has a distorted view of love. It points to a movie screen where two people are making out and calls that love. But the Bible points to Jesus, stretching His arms out wide on a cross, paying for our sin, and offering us grace and forgiveness and eternal life.

> Dear friends, let us love one another, for love comes from God. Everyone who loves has been born of God and knows God. Whoever does not love does not know God, because God is love. This is how God showed his love among us: He sent his one and only Son into the world that we might live through him. This is love: not that we loved God, but that he loved us and sent his Son as an atoning sacrifice for our sins. Dear friends, since God so loved us, we also ought to love one another.... And so we know and rely on the love God has for us. God is love. Whoever lives in love lives in God, and God in them. This is how love is made complete among us so that we will have confidence on the day of judgment: In this world we are like Jesus. There is no fear in love. But perfect love drives out fear, because fear has to do with punishment. The one who fears is not made perfect in love. (1 John 4:7–11, 16–18)

We tell people to face their fears. But we don't need to face our fears—instead we need to turn and face God and receive His love. We don't need to fear, because God is with us. And we don't even need to fear Judgment Day, because Jesus gave His life for us.

In 2 Corinthians 5:21, we see that God made Him who knew no

sin to become sin so that we might become the righteousness of God in Christ. God the Father treated Jesus on the cross as if He had sinned. Jesus took on all the sin of the world. So that now, when we place our faith in Jesus, God the Father looks at us as if we have lived a perfect life. In other words, Jesus copied and pasted His life over ours. He exchanged His perfect life for our sinful one. It's the great exchange.

You don't need to fear in this life or the life to come when you follow Jesus and receive God's amazing love. Fear has got to go. It has no choice and cannot stay anymore. So, again, if you're struggling with fear, don't get more bold—get more love. Begin to set your mind on how deep and how wide and how high and how great His love is for you, and then simply respond to that love by surrendering the control of your life to Him. The fear that has kept you in the dip, that is indeed strong, will then be kicked out by something stronger: God's perfect love.

Don't get more bold—get more love. Begin to set your mind on how deep and how wide and how high and how great His love is for you.

ADOPTED

Perhaps you've heard the story of a young boy who was teased for being adopted. Every day, on his way home from school, the same group of bullies made fun of him. As he walked down his street, those boys would begin to laugh and point as they hurled insults surrounding the fact that he was adopted. This led to the young boy feeling insecure, less than, and afraid to even walk down his own street.

But one day as he was sitting in class, it all changed. A new thought occurred to him. This day, he couldn't wait to see those boys. What he normally dreaded, today he anticipated. As he stood up by the door, watching the second hand on the clock lead up to the bell to dismissal, and with his backpack slung over his shoulders, he exited the classroom and headed home like a man on a mission.

As always, those boys were on his street corner, and they started up again, as they had done every day for weeks. "You're adopted! You're adopted!" But this time, instead of trying to avoid the harassment by walking on the other side of the street, the little boy crossed the street and walked directly up to the group of bullies. With his shaky voice, oversize backpack, and newfound boldness, he lifted up his finger and said, "Every day you guys make fun of me because I'm adopted. Well, I've been doing some thinking. My parents wanted me so badly they got on a plane and flew to another country. They had to pay thousands of dollars, take time off from work, and out of all the little kids in the orphanage, they *chose* me! Your parents didn't have a choice!" And with that the boys shut up, the little boy smiled as he walked home, and they never bothered him again.

Listen, God loves you so much! He went to great lengths to show you His love, and He doesn't want you living in fear and anxiety. Romans 8:15 promises, "The Spirit you received does not make you slaves, so that you live in fear again; rather, the Spirit you received brought about your adoption to sonship. And by Him we cry, 'Abba, Father.'" God has now adopted you as a son or a daughter of God, so you can now call Him "Abba Father." *Abba* is the first word a little Hebrew child would learn to call their dad. In other words, it's like calling Him "Dada." And with the innocence restored, and the covering of our heavenly Father's love and acceptance, we now have a confidence and a peace with His almighty protection. God. Loves. You.

When I was around ten, I remember walking down the street and picking a flower. As I began to pull one petal off at a time, I'd say, "She loves me." Then I'd pull another petal off and say, "She loves me not." Another petal, "She loves me." The next petal, "She loves me not." I'd do that until I got all the way down to the last petal, hoping it landed on

"She loves me." If the last petal was "She loves me not," I would improvise, of course, and count the stem as "She loves me!" while tossing it over my shoulder.

I think that's how we sometimes view God. We think, *He loved me on Thursday. He doesn't love me today. He loves me. He loves me not. He loves me when I'm doing good. He doesn't love me when I'm doing bad.* We think God's love is like human love. But it's not.

If we were taking petals off a flower, it would be, "He loves me! He loves me! He loves me! He loves me!" His love never changes. His love never shifts. His love never dwindles. His love never fades. His love is consistent, perfect, and never-ending. And according to Romans 8:38–39, *nothing* can separate us from the love of God!

God's love will lift you out of the dip, but you've got to leave fear in the dip. It's not coming with you, because once God's love fills you, there isn't any more room for fear!

Chapter 17

PUT THE SHOVEL DOWN

In 1649, during the English Civil War, a powerful politician named Oliver Cromwell plotted to overthrow the monarchy under the rule of King Charles I with his political party. Their victory over the Royalist Party was swift, and they tried King Charles I for treason against his country. It was a novel idea to actually try a king, but fifty-nine people signed a document for King Charles' execution, and it was granted.

Eleven years later, when the Royalist Party came into power again, the first order of business for King Charles II was bringing to trial the fifty-nine people who had signed the death warrant for his father. The only problem was that the mastermind behind his father's execution, Oliver Cromwell, was already dead. So were a few others.

King Charles II tried and convicted dozens of men and sentenced them to be tortured, quartered, and hanged. But that wasn't good enough. He ordered that the bodies of Oliver Cromwell, along with two others, be dug up and hanged too! They actually unearthed buried corpses and tried them in front of a jury as if they were still alive! But this *still* was not enough. He had the heads of Cromwell and the other two lopped off and mounted on twenty-foot spikes above Westminster Hall, where King Charles I had been tried. There the three skulls decorated the English skyline for more than twenty years!

Talk about digging up your past. That's a crazy picture of what happens when we don't deal with forgiveness the right way. I heard Chris Hodges talk about this once, pointing out how this historical account sounds so extreme, and yet we all know what it's like to carry a shovel around in life, ready to dig up old hurts and offenses. We take our shovel with us to our job. We bring it with us into every relationship and into our church. With every dig, we remember how others treated us. Even though 1 Corinthians 13:4 says that love "keeps no record of wrongs," some of us have a filing cabinet filled with precise records of how people have wronged us. We remember the exact day they said what they said. We remember the tone in which they said it. We rehearse the pain they caused. We have become obsessed with the archaeological dig of our past wounds, and instead of walking into our future with freedom, we are stuck in our dip and digging ourselves deeper and deeper. With our own shovel. And we don't even realize it.

Instead of walking into our future, we are stuck wandering around in our past, carrying a shovel. But our shovels cannot fit through the doors of our destinies. Offended people never make it to their destiny. If we want to get out of the dip, then it's time to PUT THE SHOVEL DOWN! Forgiveness helps us climb out of the dip.

HOW JESUS FORGAVE

Jesus sets the bar high when it comes to forgiveness. I agree with Jack Hayford: as Christ followers, we desire to reflect His character in all things, including forgiveness. If that's the case, we are going to need to study how He did it. In *The Message* Bible, we read these great words:

> Do you see what this means—all these pioneers who blazed the way, all these veterans cheering us on? It means we'd better get on with it. Strip down, start running—and never quit! No extra spiritual fat, no parasitic sins. Keep your eyes on Jesus, who both began and finished this race we're in. *Study how he did it.* Because he never lost sight of where he was headed—that exhilarating finish in and with God—he could put up with anything along the way: Cross, shame, whatever. And now he's there, in the place of honor, right alongside God. When you find yourselves flagging in your faith, go over that story again, item by item, that long litany of hostility he plowed through. That will shoot adrenaline into your souls! (Hebrews 12:1–3, emphasis mine)

Any dip you and I ever face is nothing compared to what Jesus experienced on His worst day. We call it "Good Friday," but it was only good for us. It was a horrible day for Jesus, which He didn't even deserve. But He was still able to forgive. Let's do as these verses in Hebrews exhort us to do: let's study how Jesus did it.

It began on Thursday night for Jesus when He was illegally tried. It was against the law in both Roman and Jewish courts to try somebody at night. He tolerated three exhausting trials in front of several different leaders. He endured torture of the worst kind. He was whipped and beaten. His skull was gouged with a crown made of thorns as a mockery. And then He was nailed to a cross. Those spikes didn't go into His hands as we imagine, either. Roman executioners used to place the nail there, but they found people could wiggle free. If you take your fingers and feel the empty spot above your wrist, in between the two bones, that's where they drove the spikes.

Around nine in the morning they hoisted the cross, and as He hung there—an innocent man who had committed zero crimes—He uttered this statement: "Father, forgive them, for they do not know what they are doing" (Luke 23:34).

Are you kidding me? That's probably the last thing that we'd say in that position. I would've been calling lightning down from heaven on everybody. "You're dead. He's dead. Dead! Dead! Dead! All y'all are dead!" You and I lose it in traffic! But here was Jesus, hanging on a cross in physical agony, forgiving all. Even more shocking was the fact that this was the *first* thing He said. Forgiveness is a big deal to Him.

In what we call the Lord's Prayer, when Jesus was teaching the disciples how to pray, He included, "forgive us our sins, as we have forgiven those who sin against us" (Matthew 6:12). Did you catch that? "Forgive us, *as we forgive*." I heard Robert Morris explain that this means "to the same degree as." "With the same measure as." You might be thinking, *What's the big deal?* Well, we may have been praying judgment on ourselves for years without even knowing it. We've basically been asking God, "Lord, would you forgive me with the same measure that I forgive other people?" Think about it. Do we really want God to use the way we forgive other people as a barometer for how He forgives us?

We must learn to put the shovel down and forgive. The truth is people are going to hurt you. It's going to happen. And you still need to learn to forgive *completely*. I know what some of you are thinking. *Ouch! Shaun, why can't you be more positive?* All right, I'm *positive* people are going to hurt you. And I'm *positive* that you still need to learn to forgive completely. Offenses and hurts are sure to come, but you have the choice whether or not you stay in that space of pain.

> Offenses and hurts are sure to come, but you have the choice whether or not you stay in that space of pain.

Jesus said, "It is impossible that no offenses should come, but woe to him through whom they do come!" (Luke 17:1 NKJV). When we get offended, we hold on to unforgiveness, as if by doing so we're punishing the other person. We think, *I'll show them.* But we're not showing them anything. Look at the logic we use. It's like we're saying, "I'll get back at them. I'll live a horrible life, derailed by offense, and that'll show them!"

Listen, they don't care. They've moved on. And yet that offense is destroying you and keeping you in the dip. Forgiveness is a must if we want to get out of the dip. We hold on to toxic memories. Why do we tend to remember what we're supposed to forget and forget what we're supposed to remember? When Jesus forgives, He forgets (Hebrews 8:12). We say, "I'll forgive them but I will never forget." That way is not true forgiveness. In your forgiveness don't forget to forget. I'll tell you how.

WEEDING OUT BITTERNESS

Hebrews 12:15 offers us this command: "See to it that no one falls short of the grace of God and that no bitter root grows up to cause trouble and defile many." The Bible describes bitterness as a bitter root. Have you ever looked at your backyard and seen some weeds growing? You think to yourself, *I should deal with that*, but you don't. The weeds are so small anyway, but after you procrastinate for a week, it seems like they've grown to be six feet tall. What started off as something that could have been easily dealt with has now become Jack and the beanstalk in your backyard.

When you have just a small weed with a small root, it's easy to handle. You just pull it out of the ground with no problems. But when you wait too long, you pull and pull, straining and struggling, to no avail. It's as if the roots are a mile deep into the earth. The longer you let a weed grow, the harder it is to get rid of. If you've ever tried to pull out a big root, you know it's backbreaking work, and many times you end up breaking it off and you think you're good. You think, *Phew! Glad that's over. I'm done with it!* Outta sight, outta mind. But if you don't get the entire root, there's a whole lot more going on beneath the surface that you can't see—and when it grows back, you'll have to dig up more than you were anticipating because now you have a jungle of overgrowth to tackle as its roots have spread.

If you don't *completely* uproot bitterness now, those roots will go down so deep they will latch on and interweave their way into every relationship you have. Bitterness will affect your view of everything you see. And it will keep you from the destiny God has for you to walk in. It's a trap! Why give somebody or a particular situation that much power over your life? It's been three years. It's messed with you for ten years. It's kept you from enjoying life for twenty years. It's stolen your joy for thirty-two years. It's kept you from so much in life, and now you feel like you can't move on. Why not determine today not to allow it to rob you of one more day of your life? Better yet, refuse to get offended ever again.

If anybody had reasons to become offended, it was Jesus. He was betrayed by almost everyone in His life, and yet He still forgave because He knew that He couldn't fulfill His destiny any other way. He had to show us what we would one day be able to do through Him. He was revealing to us a lesson in forgiveness. Had He not forgiven, He would have been just another man dying on a cross. But through this ultimate act of forgiveness, He gained victory over bitterness and death, and He now gives us the power to do the same.

CHANGE YOUR THINKING

Forgiveness is not saying what they did was okay. It wasn't okay, and that's why it hurt. When our daughters were young, and one would do something to upset another, I would tell the offender, "Say you're sorry." And with her head down, she would quietly say, "Sorry." To which the other would say, "It's okay." This is where I'd correct them. "No, it's not okay. It wasn't okay that your sisters tied sheets around your neck and then the three of them went up to the second-story balcony and tried to hoist you up. That's actually not okay." By the way, that's a true story, which they just told us about recently. There are some things you don't tell your parents until you're grown. This is one of them. I told them, "Don't say 'It's okay.' Say 'I forgive you.'"

Forgiveness is not trusting someone automatically again. For instance, if you were abused by someone when you were a child, now that you are an adult, you're not going to let them babysit your kids. But you can forgive that abuser. Even if that person never apologizes. Listen. You can forgive and never get an "I'm sorry" because you don't need it to forgive. Remember, we are studying how Jesus did it. Nobody who whipped Him, or condemned Him, or nailed Him to the cross apologized; to the contrary, they were shouting insults and mocking Him. Yet He still said, "Father, forgive them, for they don't know what they're doing."

You might say, "But they don't deserve it!" Well, neither did we, but I'm really grateful God didn't wait till we *deserved* it. Instead, He gave us forgiveness even when we didn't deserve it. Forgiveness is not about being fair. It's about grace, giving us something that we don't deserve. It's about mercy, withholding the judgment that we do deserve. And all of this is motivated by His amazing, unfathomable love, which He showed in this way: "While we were still sinners, Christ died for us" (Romans 5:8).

You might say, "But they don't deserve it!" Well, neither did we, but I'm really grateful God didn't wait till we *deserved* it.

Why is it we want to judge others by their actions, but we want others to judge us by our intentions? We sure want mercy from others, but then how is it that we have a hard time giving it? Extending forgiveness, even to those we feel do not deserve it, is not impossible. With God's help, you can do this, but first you have to put the shovel down and move on. Most of us have a hard time forgiving because we don't want to *give them* anything. I want to share with you a picture God gave me to help me think differently about forgiveness.

I'm on top of a tall skyscraper in San Francisco. I have a long, thick rope tied around my waist. At the other end of the rope is a piano that has just been pushed off the side of the building. It's only a matter of seconds before all the slack is gone and the piano pulls me over the edge. I really want to hold on to the piano, but I'll die if I do. See, most of us have a hard time forgiving others because, in our minds, we don't want to give them anything, but forgiveness is not about giving them something. It's releasing something. It's me, untying the rope from around my waist, choosing life over death, because if I don't, that piano will pull me over the edge.

That might be where you are. That bitterness is pulling you over the edge. It's killing you. It's hindering you. It's keeping you from living the John 10:10 life Jesus came to bring. You can't focus on living when you're just trying not to be pulled over the edge. You can't get close to anyone when you're just trying not to be pulled over. So untie the rope and release it. Release the offense. Release your pain. Release feelings of revenge. And experience the freedom that comes through complete forgiveness. Forgive them and put the shovel down.

TORMENTED IN THE DIP

I heard Robert Morris say, "Forgiveness is bringing their balance to zero." This is when you're not expecting them to pay you back. That's what we're waiting for, right? This is why we hold on to unforgiveness and bitterness, because we want them to pay us back. But if you bring their balance to zero, this releases them because you're not expecting any payment from them. And by releasing them it also releases you.

Peter once asked Jesus, "Lord, how often should I forgive someone who sins against me? Seven times?" (Matthew 18:21 NLT). In this culture, three was the number required. So Peter thought he'd double it and add one. Peter was always trying to show off. But Jesus answered,

"Seventy times seven." By this Jesus wasn't being literal, saying 490, as if at 491 times you were free to pounce. He was saying we shouldn't keep count because He knows what that does to us. Then Jesus went on to tell Peter a story to help all of us understand better.

There was a guy who owed his boss a lot of money. When he couldn't pay, his boss ordered that the man be thrown into prison and his family sold into slavery. In this era, you didn't just file for bankruptcy and move on. No, when you couldn't pay your debt, you went to prison and they'd confiscate your kids and make them slaves. If this were the standard today, I don't think we'd see so much credit card debt. The guy in debt begged his boss for mercy, and the boss relented mercifully, forgiving the *entire* debt. Can you imagine what a relief that must have been to the man and his family? Later, though, that same guy who had been forgiven came across another guy who owed him a little bit of money and put him in a choke hold, demanding that he pay him back. The man begged for mercy, but it was not given, and so the man who owed hardly anything was thrown in prison!

When word got back to the original boss, he called in this guy and said, "You wicked servant! I forgave you all that debt because you begged me. Should you not also have had compassion on your fellow servant, just as I had pity on you?" (Matthew 18:32–33 NKJV). The boss was so angry that he turned him over to the jailers to be tormented until he could pay back all he owed. Jesus then told His disciples, "This is how my heavenly Father will treat each of you unless you forgive your brother or sister from your heart" (Matthew 18:35).

That forgiven but unforgiving man was handed over to be tormented. There are some people who have been tormented because they refuse to forgive. If that's you, for your sake release them! It's like you're sitting in a prison cell with the keys to get out, but you refuse to open the cell. Jesus couldn't have been clearer when he said, "If you forgive other people when they sin against you, your heavenly Father will also forgive you. But if you do not forgive others their sins, your Father will not forgive your sins" (Matthew 6:14–15).

We love the first part, but that second part is scary. God is serious about you putting the shovel down. Maybe you're feeling distant from God. Could it be a bitter root, an unforgiven offense that has led to you feeling isolated from God, and now you're feeling tormented in a dip?

You've got to let it go. Release them. Jesus couldn't have completed His calling if He didn't do this, and neither will you. Forgive them as unto Jesus. Matthew 10:8 exhorts us, "Freely you have received; freely give." Why do we always want to charge people for what we got for free? Why do we want to make people work for what we got for free? If Jesus gave it to us for free, we ought to pass it on! And the reason it's easier to forgive now is because we've been forgiven. We'll never have to forgive anyone more than Jesus has forgiven us.

Forgive as Jesus forgave. Remember, they're broken. And broken people do broken things. Just like healed people do healed things. The forgiven forgive. If you don't forgive, you will keep the cycle going and create a legacy of bitterness for generations. Which cycle do you want to keep going—one that creates a legacy of bitterness for generations to come, or one that gives hope and healing from now through eternity?

You can be free. It's time to put the shovel down. Bring their balance to zero. Get out of the dip and start living again. Whisper right now to God and tell Him, "I forgive," and say their name. This is not about feeling it. It's a choice and it's about releasing them because Jesus released you. And the dip of bitterness will hold you no more.

Chapter 18

DESTROYING THE HAMSTER WHEEL

Most humans love having pets. Not my dad, though. Growing up, I would frequently ask my parents for a pet. On one particular day, I was determined not to take no for an answer. "Can I have a dog?" Dad, unsurprisingly, said no. I thought I'd disarm him with cleverness. "How about a ferret?" He wasn't amused. Then I got really desperate and asked for a cat. Dad said no. I was quiet for a minute and finally asked, "Can I have something with four legs?" So my dad bought me a chair. His name was Max. He was a good chair. I taught him to sit. I'm kidding.

I finally wore my dad down. (That's one of my spiritual gifts—just ask Dianna, who finally said yes after the tenth proposal.) So my dad offered to buy me a hamster, probably just to shut me up. It wasn't a dog, but I said, "I'll take it." I named him B&W because he was brown and white.

My dad and I bought all the things my hamster needed, including the plastic exercise ball in which B-Dub could run all around the house on our hardwood floors. He loved that! Well, he loved it until the day my dad walked into the house and "accidentally" kicked the hamster ball, midstride, like an Olympic soccer player. That hamster had the ride of his life, flying across the room, tumbling and spinning with g-forces he had never experienced before. When the ball finally came to a stop, I could've sworn I saw his tiny front paws go up, as if to say, "Yeahhh! Let's do it again!"

Here are some interesting facts about hamsters you probably didn't know:

1. Their teeth never stop growing.
2. They have large cheeks in which they can carry food home. Wouldn't that be helpful at a buffet? A waitress asks if you'd like a to-go box, and you're like, "No, I'm good. I'm just gonna shove this pizza in my cheeks for later."
3. They can have up to twenty babies in a litter. Their gestation period is sixteen to thirty days. But they've also been known to eat their offspring. Isn't that crazy?!
4. Once a hamster gives birth, it can get pregnant again that same day. All the women get mad at this one.
5. Their name is from the German word *hamstern*, which means "to hoard."
6. They are solitary to a fault. They will fight others to the death.
7. They have really bad vision.
8. They run. A lot. This is probably what they are best known for. In the wild they can run six to thirteen miles a night. They're serious about their cardio.

Every hamster cage has a hamster wheel. You can't buy a cage without one. Hamsters, which were created to run and explore, have learned to settle for running on the hamster wheel. Can you imagine putting in a full day's work, for eight hours, running six to thirteen miles...but never getting anywhere? You start and stop in the same place, every day. So you're exhausted, but not productive.

AN ENDLESS CYCLE

I wonder if you've ever felt like that, as though your life is just going in circles. Where you know you were created to grow, possess, and make a difference and yet you've settled for a comfortable, familiar pattern. A boring rut. A dip.

All of us can get stuck in a season where we are not growing. Not advancing. Not risking. Not believing. Sure, we're busy (some of us don't know how to be anything else, but that's a different lesson), but with all our activity there is no progression. Our life has become nothing more than a hamster wheel. It's not what we set out to accomplish, but at least it's safe and familiar. At least we know what to expect. So we put in our eight hours a day. We come home tired but not fulfilled, busy but not fruitful. We're stuck in a repetitive cycle, and we are bored to death with the monotonous rut.

We tell ourselves, "Well, at least I'm being faithful." Wait a second. Let's not kid ourselves. Faithfulness is not faithfulness unless fruitfulness is involved. Jesus told the story of a boss going on a trip and he gave his three servants bags filled with gold. To one he gave five bags. To the other he gave two. And to the last, he gave one. When he came back, he wanted to see the return on investment with these guys. The guy with five said, "I doubled it." The guy with two said, "I doubled it." The guy with one said, "I hid it in the ground and I'm giving back to you what you gave me." The boss said, "You wicked and lazy servant." And then he took the one bag that the man had and gave it to the guy who now had ten. The only guys to whom he said, "Well done, good and *faithful* servant," were the two guys who did something with what they were given (Matthew 25:14–30).

Now, not all routine is bad. Some doctors have said that going to bed and waking up at the same time every day is good for you. Praying every morning is a must. Kissing your spouse before you leave every morning is a great routine. Exercise is good for you. Routines can be beneficial. Ruts are not. A routine helps us be at our best. A rut prevents us from moving forward.

In the Bible, the people of Israel were in a colossal rut. It was so deep that they were stuck in it for forty years. The book of Numbers describes the entire forty-year rut, but for the sake of time, let's just go to the recap found in Deuteronomy 2:1. Look how sad this verse is: "Then we turned around and headed back across the wilderness toward the Red Sea, just as the LORD had instructed me, and we wandered around in the region of Mount Seir *for a long time*" (NLT, emphasis mine).

This is that moment when you're sitting in a movie theater and you start yelling at the characters on the screen, "You're turning *back*?! To go to the very place God just delivered you from? Y'all are crazy! NOOO!" And as I talked about earlier in this book, things just got worse for the Israelites. Once they finally sent spies to check out the Promised Land, they bought into all the negative news and rejected the faith of Caleb and Joshua, who tried to convince them what life could be like. The people basically said, "That looks incredible, but...we'll pass." Failing to trust God and all their murmuring and complaining didn't go well for the people, as we read in Deuteronomy 1:35–36: "No one from this evil generation shall see the good land I swore to give your ancestors, except Caleb.... He will see it, and I will give him and his descendants the land he set his feet on, because he followed the LORD wholeheartedly." (Of course, we know from other verses that God also praised Joshua for his faith and appointed him to lead the people into the Promised Land.)

What was the wilderness? It was a big ol' hamster wheel. They knew their Nikes wouldn't wear out. Their North Face robe would be just fine. They trusted God would give them Wonder bread each morning. It wasn't the Promised Land, but it was familiar. They were content just looking at the promise but weren't willing to get off their hamster wheel. For forty years they went round and round on that hamster wheel. Round and round that mountain. They'd get off for a brief look, take a quick selfie, and then jump right back on their hamster wheel. Right back into the dip. They thought they'd just have a little trip into the wilderness for a while to regroup, but that ended up being forty years. Don't you hate it when you become a prisoner of that which you thought you would just be a visitor?

We love Joshua and Caleb. We preach sermons about them. We name our sons after them. They were the only ones who believed the promise of God and could see it as a possible future. And then one day I felt like God said to me, "And that was also their problem." Wait. What? What do you mean, God? He then explained it to me:

How is it that out of a million-plus people, Caleb and Joshua couldn't find *one other person* to see what they saw? They couldn't convince anyone else to believe along with them? It is so important that we realize this is not just about you getting off your hamster wheel; this is about you helping other people see why they should get off theirs too.

It's easy to point fingers, but their struggle is one we can relate to, because all of us have areas where we've stagnated. Areas in which we might be bored, but at least we know what to expect. And so we circle and circle and circle...But when we circle, our faith begins to atrophy and weaken because we believe we don't need to rely on God to get through our day. We settle. Instead of believing God for more, we cling to our hamster wheel.

The devil wants to convince you to be satisfied with the desolate desert instead of your desired destiny, wandering busily instead of possessing; but movement is not the same as progress. Are you getting this? The hamster wheel is a distraction. It makes you *think* you're going places when you're really just maintaining. And the distraction is a counterfeit, an imitation of something valuable, and its purpose is to deceive.

When I was eighteen and went to New York City, I bought a Rolex watch for $20. I thought to myself, *Wow! Prices have really come down.* It broke before I got home to California because it was a counterfeit. The devil would love to convince you that your hamster wheel is as good as God's promise. He would love to get you to be satisfied with a cheap imitation of God's plan. He wants to trick you into thinking that you can pay a lower price and still receive the same quality. It's a great distraction technique.

> Movement is not the same as progress... It makes you *think* you're going places when you're really just maintaining.

If the devil can't get you to quit in the dip, he'll get you distracted. A distracted leader is just as bad as a quitting leader because both stop moving forward. It doesn't matter to the devil which one you are because to him, both stop building. And both stop moving in God's direction. Remember Solomon? He was on a hamster wheel too.

> "Meaningless! Meaningless!" says the Teacher. "Utterly meaningless! Everything is meaningless." What do people gain from all their labors at which they toil under the sun? Generations come and generations go, but the earth remains forever. The sun rises and the sun sets, and hurries back to where it rises. The wind blows to the south and turns to the north; round and round it goes, ever returning on its course. All streams flow into the sea, yet the sea is never full. To the place the streams come from, there they return again. All things are wearisome, more

> than one can say. The eye never has enough of seeing, nor the ear its fill of hearing. (Ecclesiastes 1:1–8)

This is coming from a guy who had it all! He was the king. He had all the money and power that anyone could imagine, and yet he was so miserable on his hamster wheel. Nothing could satisfy. If you read his book, it's super depressing. It's just him trying to find purpose in everything except God for twelve chapters. At the end, he sums it all up by saying, "Here's the conclusion of the matter; fear God and keep His commandments" (Ecclesiastes 12:13). That's it!

After the Israelites had been going around the mountain for so long, we're told, "Then at last the LORD said to me, 'You have been wandering around in this hill country long enough; turn to the north'" (Deuteronomy 2:2–3 NLT). Where do you find yourself just going through the motions? Where are you just maintaining? Where do you feel like you've just been going in circles, around and around? Maybe God's getting your attention in this book to let you know, "You have gone around this mountain long enough." It's time to realize that your *wheel* is not God's *will.*

Maybe it's time to tell God, "Not my *wheel*, but Your *will* be done." Tell Him, "God, I'm tired of coasting and simply maintaining. I'm done just running in circles. I'm choosing to surrender it all again. To trust You again. To put You first and believe You again. God, today I'm destroying my hamster wheel!"

Maybe text somebody right now and tell them, "I'm destroying my hamster wheel." Decide that you're not just going to go through the motions anymore and that there's purpose inside of you. There's greatness inside of you. There's destiny inside of you that maybe you haven't seen because you've only been focusing on your hamster wheel. Why would you settle for looking at the promise when you can walk into it?

HELP OTHERS GET OFF THEIR WHEEL

It breaks my heart to see people with so much potential refuse to get off their hamster wheel. I'm here to wake you up because you might be falling asleep at the wheel. Wake up! It's time to destroy what's been keeping you from God's will, and to help others find freedom and purpose as well.

Why would you settle for looking at the promise when you can walk into it?

I'm grateful for all the people who destroyed their hamster wheels. Great men and women of God who wanted to quit in the dip but didn't. People who felt stuck in a rut but pressed through and climbed out. They could've easily stayed on their hamster wheel, but they didn't. They destroyed it and began walking into the promise God had for them. And because they did, my life has been so greatly impacted by theirs.

Who's waiting for you on the other side of your hamster wheel?

Don't stay on the hamster wheel. You were created to run with intentionality and purpose, not around in circles. Destroy the hamster wheel.

SECTION SIX

Chapter 19

WHAT YOU SEE IS NOT ALWAYS WHAT YOU GET

We live in a world that is constantly sizing people up. I did it this week. I was walking down the street, encountered someone for the first time, and immediately made a judgment about them based on a first impression. You probably do this too. It's human nature, isn't it? We've all judged a book by its cover: at school, at a store, at work, even at church. We glance at someone and immediately judgments flash through our minds. But let me ask you a question: Have you ever been wrong?

Have you ever looked at someone and thought, *They can't play basketball,* and then they beat you? Have you ever seen someone walk up to the mic on one of those reality singing shows and thought, *They can't sing,* and then they blow your mind? Have you ever looked at someone and thought, *They look mean,* and then they become your best friend? Sometimes we are surprised at the outcome because our own preconceived notions don't allow us to see that there is more than meets the eye.

In the Old Testament, God told Samuel to go to the house of a guy named Jesse, and there he was to anoint—which means "to choose and set apart"—one of Jesse's sons to be the next king of Israel.

I'm sure you can imagine the excitement in the family when Samuel arrived. He was a celebrity prophet whose presence commanded awe. Then, to have Samuel announce that one of their family members was going to be the next king, the suspense would've been palpable. Everybody automatically assumed the favored son would be the oldest. I mean, if anyone deserved it, in this culture, it should be the firstborn son, right? Samuel sized up this handsome, burly young man and made an immediate judgment in favor of him, until God clearly spoke to his heart: "He's not the one." This was quite a shock to the family. I bet the second-oldest son started to feel the rush of excitement as he thought, *I didn't think it'd be me, but maybe it should be.* He was summoned into the living room with Samuel, and God said, "He's not the one either." Then God gave further direction to Samuel:

> The LORD said to Samuel, "Do not consider his appearance or his height, for I have rejected him. The LORD does not look at the things people look at. People look at the outward appearance, but the LORD looks at the heart."
>
> Then Jesse called Abinadab and had him pass in front of Samuel. But Samuel said, "The LORD has not chosen this one either." Jesse then had Shammah pass by, but Samuel said, "Nor has the LORD chosen this one." Jesse had seven of his sons pass before Samuel, but Samuel said to him, "The LORD has not chosen these." So he asked Jesse, "Are these all the sons you have?" (1 Samuel 16:7–11)

The brothers were thinking, *Well, there is* one *more…but it's just David.* They probably laughed under their breath. They had to tell the prophet, "We didn't even invite him to the party. He's out in the field watching sheep." But Samuel, not fazed by their disregard for the last son, said, "Send for him; we will not sit down until he arrives."

That would have been an awkward forty-five minutes.

"Samuel, would you like to sit down?"

"No."

"Would you like something to eat?"

"No."

"Can we at least get you a cup of water?"

Samuel was too preoccupied looking out the window, waiting. Scripture says that when David finally arrived, "he was glowing with health and had a fine appearance and handsome features. Then the LORD said, 'Rise and anoint him; this is the one'" (1 Samuel 16:12).

Even David's own father didn't believe in him. Wow. It's pretty hurtful when your own family overlooks you. But if you're going to be used by God, sometimes you have to learn to be okay with knowing you are anointed and yet not accepted. There are times when you know you have a calling on your life, but your family doesn't see it yet. I'm sure Jesus had many days in His three decades on earth when He felt misunderstood and condemned by His own family.

You might have thought to yourself, *I think God's given me some pretty big dreams, but when I shared them with a few people, they looked at me like I was crazy.* Because of their responses, you might have started to think there is no way God could ever use you. Don't allow these negative voices to limit you. In fact, don't ever view your calling through the lens of someone else's limitations. This view will only cause you to start categorizing yourself in a different way—the wrong way. You'll start to think that God only uses superstar believers but not you. You'll be tempted to think, *God would rather use someone else, in another city, with a big*

Don't ever view your calling through the lens of someone else's limitations.

following on social media. He surely won't use me. I'm a nobody. Well, God always uses people who feel like nobodies. You're not a nobody to Him. He loves you. He values you. And He often shows His grace through people who are unassuming. Sometimes what we overlook is actually attractive to God. May I remind you, God does not look at people the way man looks at them.

GOD MAKES NOBODIES SOMEBODIES

Why would God choose a nobody? God always picks a nobody. God never picks a somebody. Why? Because when God uses a nobody, He gets all the credit and all the glory. Everybody steps back and says, "It wasn't their talent. It wasn't their ability. They can't even really sing. That boy can barely preach. But I'm telling you, when they open their mouth, the hand of God is on them and God uses them in such powerful ways!" When God picks you, He chooses you for a reason; then He prepares you for something that you cannot handle right now!

What you see is not always what you get! Sometimes it's our own reflection in the mirror that we've sized up with a wrong conclusion, and we judge ourselves as nobodies. If you've ever felt like a nobody, welcome to the club! God's entire church is filled with nobodies, but we're dedicated and dependent on God. What you see is not always what you get.

You may not look like much, but then again, neither did Moses, a baby floating down the river in a wicker basket from a craft store. But God would use him to deliver a million-plus people from slavery.

Joseph didn't look like much. He was sold into slavery by his own brothers. Falsely accused. Thrown in prison. Forgotten. But God would elevate him to be the second in command of the most powerful nation in the world at that time—Egypt. And God would give him a strategy to save thousands of people's lives.

Noah didn't look like much. But God used him to build a boat, without a Home Depot in sight, that would save his entire family.

Esther didn't look like much, but with a quiver in her lip and a hesitation in her step, she would be used to save her entire people from annihilation.

Peter didn't look like much. He would deny that he even knew Jesus, but God would restore him and use him to preach the first sermon of the early church, where three thousand people would give their lives to Jesus in one day, and he would go on to become one of the greatest leaders.

Paul didn't look like much to the early church. He hated Christians and then he became one. He would then go on to become the greatest missionary the world has ever seen and write one-third of our New Testament.

Jesus didn't look like much in a borrowed horse trough, but He would go on to become the Savior of the world! You might not look like much right now, but I'm telling you, God chooses the foolish things of the world to confound the wise. What you see is not always what you get!

START SMALL

When our daughters were young, and they were getting ready to take their first steps, Dianna and I were so excited. We were there for each one, with our big video camera poised on one shoulder, because this was before the smartphone. We held our breath as we waited, anticipating their first steps. And when they finally took their first step, it wasn't even a good one. Our baby girls didn't take off and walk around the block or run to the store and back. It was one off-balance, awkward step before they dropped to the ground.

But when they took that first step, we lost our minds. It was as monumental to us as Neil Armstrong's first step on the moon. I began to scream! "Ohhh, that's my girl! Did you see that? Send a copy of that video to everybody! She's so advanced for her age!" And it was just one small step. Can I tell you that when you take one small step toward God and your calling, all of heaven rejoices and your heavenly Father says, "Ohhh, that's My girl! That's My son!" In Zechariah 4:10, He encourages us with this verse: "Do not despise these small beginnings, for the LORD rejoices to see the work begin" (NLT).

Even if you feel like you don't look like much right now, there's a little word that God tucked deep into your soul: *potential.* God looks at you and sees every possibility *and* complete capability to develop into all He desires for you. It's just that sometimes we look at our beginning steps and we downplay them because we feel they are not significant enough. God does not see as you see.

We live in an era when people are obsessed with instant results. We expect to step out and immediately have an incredible impact on the world. But God often says to us, "Whoa, slow down." We feel like our dream is going to be fulfilled tomorrow and it's usually not. But don't get discouraged.

He wants to do exceedingly abundantly above all you can ask or think, according to the power of God that works inside of you (Ephesians 3:20), and it all starts with a small step. It all begins with the seed of potential that He's placed in your heart. I know your dream may seem too big right now, and that's okay. God's dream is always bigger than your own.

I know your dream may seem too big right now, and that's okay. God's dream is always bigger than your own.

Let me explain it this way. Growing up, were you ever given hand-me-down clothes from older siblings or cousins? And you never liked these. Why? Because they never fit! They were always too big. But what did your mom tell you? "Don't worry, you'll grow into it." Your calling will always be bigger than you at first, but with God, don't worry, you'll grow into it. God has a plan and a purpose for your life but He's waiting to see if you're willing to be developed. Trust me, you don't want to fast-forward to places where an undeveloped character is unable to handle the success. Be patient and allow God to do the developing.

DEVELOPED

There are two keys to developing in God that I want to share with you. You spend your time increasing in these areas, and you will open the doors for God to release more and more potential. One: increase your faith. Two: increase your leadership.

Hebrews 11:6 teaches us that "without faith it is impossible to please God, because anyone who comes to him must believe that he exists and that he rewards those who earnestly seek him." Faith is important to God!

Is it any wonder the devil has been attacking your faith? He knows that if he can get your faith to crumble, he wins. Hebrews didn't say it was *hard* to please God without faith. The writer said, "It's impossible." It can't happen. Why is this? Simply put, the only way to access God and His kingdom is through and by faith. Faith is a substance; it is the thing we hope for but cannot see or touch with our natural senses. God has given us all a measure of faith, and that faith can be grown!

Over the years, I've had people ask me to pray for their faith. While I can pray that their eyes will be opened and their hearts will be able to discern the things of God, that's really all I can do. Faith doesn't come by someone praying for you to get more faith. Romans 10:17 is clear that "faith comes by hearing, and hearing by the word of God" (NKJV).

If you want your faith to be developed, you need to read the Bible. If you're not reading your Bible, your faith will not grow. Don't feel like you have to read all day. Just read a little bit every day, until something stands out to you. And watch as your faith begins to grow. I've heard some people leave a church and say, "We left because we weren't being fed." What does that even mean? I'd starve too if I ate only once a week. We have more access to the Bible in this generation than we know what to do with. We have Bibles on the internet. We have Bibles in book format. There are even Bible apps that, if you're feeling too tired to read, will read for you. In a British accent! Let's not come to church saying, "Feed me. Feed me." Let's read a little every day for ourselves. I once had a friend share this thought: Last time I checked, the only people who cry when they're hungry are babies. Grown folks get up and make themselves a sandwich. Let's eat! Let's read the Bible, and the Word of God will direct you and nourish you.

Also, increase your leadership. My good friend John Maxwell said that leadership is influence. When we grow in leadership, our influence broadens in the lives of people. No matter who you are, how old you are, or what your previous experience has been, you can step out and lead another. Even if you are young, be encouraged by this: "Don't let anyone look down on you because you are young, but set an example for the believers in speech, in conduct, in love, in faith and in purity" (1 Timothy 4:12).

God's plan was that leadership would be developed in you from your youth and for you to keep growing the rest of your life. But you need to know that you have had an enemy whose plan is to try to stifle and derail that development. He goes after us, even at a young age, to try and convince us that our dreams are irrelevant, elaborate figments of our imagination. You see, the devil is not scared of who you are. He's afraid of who you might become. He knows that if you begin to correctly assess yourself the way God sees you, you will be unstoppable!

Potential is great, but it's not worth anything if it's not developed. Nurture your potential. Increase your faith and leadership. Help people move from where they are to where God wants them to be. Don't make it about you. Don't be thirsty for people to notice you. Be faithful with what God called you to. Leadership is not just about popularity and attention. God wants you to feel burdened for people. Leadership is about moving people forward. Leadership says, "Follow me. I'm going somewhere. I'll lead you to Jesus and help you develop your calling."

So, who's currently behind you? Who are you leading? One of the worst things in the world is to be stuck behind someone who's not moving. Have you ever been at a stoplight behind another car and they have their music blaring and they're on their phone? The light turns green, but they don't move.

Now, there are three kinds of people out there: ones who honk immediately to move the car in front of them, ones who give them a few-second grace period before honking, and ones who wait patiently and never honk. I'm sure I don't need to tell you which one I am. But several years ago, I drove a Honda Civic, and I wouldn't honk because I was embarrassed by the high-pitched sound of the horn.

A person says things with a horn. A strong horn tells the guy ahead of you that you mean business: "Get movin'!" But with my wimpy high-pitched Honda horn, I felt like I was the gangly junior-high boy in suspenders and head-gear braces saying in a helium-filled voice, "Um, excuse me. Excuse me. Could I possibly ask you to pay attention, if that's okay with you?" So needless to say, I wouldn't even honk. I would just sit there helpless and honkless as I waited for the car in front of me to start moving. So frustrating!

The light turns green and they just sit there. They're making a lot of noise. They're on their phone and very involved in other people's lives on social media, but when it comes to their turn they don't move!

This idea is applicable to every level of leadership. No matter if you are leading a business or a corporation, leading a small group, leading a youth group or a team in a church, or most importantly, leading in your own home, how dare we lead something that isn't moving.

Great up-and-coming leaders won't stay behind somebody who

won't move and grow. And leadership is completely measurable; it's not abstract. You can see it very easily. A title doesn't make you a leader; you don't even need a title to lead. You need leadership to lead. Some people have a title but are not good leaders. Then there are other people who don't have a title and are phenomenal leaders, because leadership is influence and helping people move from where they are to where God wants them to be. Increase your leadership.

Be dedicated to being developed. Before David was chosen, he was being developed in the fields. He was faithful with his father's sheep in the back fields. They weren't even his. He fought off a lion and a bear. God was developing him when no one else was watching. It's important for you to know that before God puts you out front, He's watching you out back. Let me take you back to the days of Bible college when I would wake up at five in the morning just to pray for an hour. Then go to school, then go to work. Then I'd stay up late writing papers, only to do it all over again. I didn't see the development at the time. Before Dianna and I stepped into our own church, we served another church, faithfully, when no one was looking. No one was calling. No one was interested. But we knew there had to be a season of preparation and development. What are you doing right now to develop yourself as a leader? It's reading, studying, praying, spending time in praise and worship to Jesus, discovering and developing your gifts and using them to serve others.

Leadership is influence and helping people move from where they are to where God wants them to be.

ORDINARY

God's working, even in the back fields of a dip. Embrace the process. A seed doesn't look like much, but with proper sunlight and water, that seed can grow to produce fruit for generations to come.

What you see is not always what you get. I don't know why God chose me. I don't say that in some sort of false humility. I really don't get it. There are many more people who are more capable, more talented, more anointed than I am. Listen. I don't know why He chose me, but I'm confident that He did. You may not understand why God chose you and that's okay, but you do need to be confident that He has.

And when God chose you, He didn't just see the insecure, wounded individual you might see in the mirror. He calls you a mighty warrior. You might be thinking, *But, Shaun, I just feel so ordinary.* We don't see God choosing a level-ten leader in the Bible. He chose level-two and level-three leaders and developed them into level-ten leaders. Let me encourage you. God always chooses ordinary people. Let me encourage you with the concept I heard Alexander James reference: One day an ordinary boy woke up feeling ordinary. This ordinary boy had an ordinary lunch and went to go see an ordinary show. And at this ordinary show, he encountered Jesus. And Jesus would take this ordinary boy's ordinary lunch and use it to feed five thousand people.

There was this ordinary woman who woke up on an ordinary day. She carried her ordinary water pot to an ordinary well. It was at this well that she met Jesus, and this ordinary woman who came to a well would turn around and become a well for her entire village to come to know Jesus.

This ordinary boy named David, who we've been talking about, who was in an ordinary field watching ordinary sheep, felt ordinary. But Samuel came into town and God told him to anoint this ordinary boy and he would go on to defeat Goliath, save his people from slavery, and become the greatest earthly king that Israel has ever known. He would write most of the psalms that encourage our hearts today.

You might have woken up today feeling ordinary, but little did you know this would be the day that God chose to get your attention to let you know you're not as ordinary as you thought you were. There's a unique calling on your life. Give your ordinary to God and watch Him work! He can take your ordinary and make it *extraordinary*. You may not look like much right now, but what you see is not always what you get!

Take a look in the mirror and ask God to show you what He sees. He sees potential and His ability on the inside of you waiting to be unleashed. Again, what you see is not always what you get. But what *God* sees can be what you get.

Chapter 20

DOMINO EFFECT

Dominoes toppling over in perfect lines are very satisfying. It's so relaxing to watch as they travel perfectly through space clicking their way to the ground. I watched a video recently that claimed to have one of the highest records for the most dominoes used in one setting: five hundred thousand. It took a team weeks to masterfully set up the many designs.

When it came time for the mega-toppling, it all started with just one domino. That first domino hit the next and the next until the entire set came alive. What started with one impacting the next moved on to one impacting several…and several impacting thousands. To see thousands toppling over to make replicas of famous paintings, like the *Mona Lisa*, was a sight to behold. That five hundred thousandth domino to be impacted was not directly touched by the first domino, but if not for the first domino, the last one never would have been impacted.

In the same way, Jesus started the domino effect. And with his life impacting twelve guys, then the twelve turned into seventy-two, then the seventy-two turned into a hundred and twenty, then three thousand. And now, here we are, two thousand years later, sitting here discussing Jesus because our lives have been impacted by those who were before us. It's the domino effect.

Most of our generation knows a man named Billy Graham. He was used to reach millions of people with the message of Jesus. He has been credited with having spoken the gospel live, in front of 215 million people in stadiums of 185 countries. That's 2.2 billion people, if you include all the radio and TV. You may know *him*, but you don't know the name of the person who led him to the Lord. We're thankful for Billy Graham, but we are also grateful for the person who told him about Jesus because if it had not been for that person, Billy would have never reached the number of people he reached.

You can't quit. People are waiting for you. What if the person who led Billy Graham to the Lord had quit in the dip? Or the person before them. There's a domino effect that God gives from one life to another. When God brings you out of the dip, it's for a reason. It's for a purpose, and that purpose is to then help other people come to know Him. I want to help you get out of the dip by helping you see what's on the other side of the dip.

When God brings you out of the dip, it's for a reason. It's for a purpose, and that purpose is to then help other people come to know Him.

A NEW PRESCRIPTION

In the last chapter, we talked many times about how what we see is not always what we get. I want to unpack that concept even further and from a different angle because in order for us to impact others, we have to see things differently. I just recently got glasses, and wow did they help me to see things differently. They also make me feel smarter. In fact, I've always wanted to have glasses, so that when I'm speaking, I can take them off in a moment when I have a good thought, and I can point the end part that goes over my ear at the crowd to really drive the point home. Props always make teaching better. Having glasses helped me to see so much better. But I'm told that every couple years I'll need to check my prescription in case it changes. Sometimes our vision changes and we need to check our prescription for our spiritual eyes so that we can see more like God sees.

Paul said, "I pray that the eyes of your heart may be enlightened in order that you may know the hope to which He has called you" (Ephesians 1:18). There's a reason behind the calling and most people never see it. How much fun would one domino be by itself? Not much at all. Dominos weren't designed to be sold in singles. They're sold in packs because they're meant to impact one another. In the same way, you are designed to impact others. If you've lost vision or clarity, I'm praying that maybe today God will change your prescription to see differently.

God sees things differently than we see them, and our goal ought to be to see things the way He does. He sees the end from the beginning, meaning He can see how the first domino will eventually impact the five hundred thousandth domino. You and I are part of that intricate and amazing plan to bring God's message of love throughout the earth, and if we don't learn to see like God sees, we will miss it. How awful would it have been if after the weeks of work spent setting up the domino display, a few dominos decided to hop out of line? The entire section after them would've been left unaffected, standing stagnant in a line.

In life, we must ask God to help us see people differently, like He sees them. For instance, picture a teenager. One person might see them as a problem. A nuisance. A bother. Jesus sees them as a son or daughter He loves. We might see a wealthy person who's always busy and think that they're full of themselves. Jesus sees a son or daughter He loves. You might see a low-income family and make judgments in your heart. Jesus sees a son or daughter He loves. You might see someone you just can't stand, maybe even someone who hurt you, but once again, Jesus sees a son or daughter He loves.

Dianna and I bought our first house when I was twenty-one years old. It was a fixer-upper in the largest sense of the word. It had no windows. No heat. No air-conditioning. There were graffiti and drug needles on the inside, just to paint you a picture. Our family members would come over to see it and they would leave crying. All they saw was a broken house, while all we saw was potential. We flipped that house. Well, actually it was more like a slow roll because it took us two years, but we made that house so cute and sold it for enough profit that it helped set us up financially at a young age.

People around you might seem like a dilapidated house. Beyond repair. But that's never how God sees them. If we don't learn to see as He sees, we will become that domino that steps out of line.

Let me show you a picture of God's heart. One day, Jesus was coming up to the city of Jerusalem, and "as he approached Jerusalem and saw the city, he wept over it and said, 'If you, even you, had only known on this day what would bring you peace—but now it is hidden from your eyes'" (Luke 19:41–42).

Why did Jesus weep? We have no record of any of His friends shedding any tears for that city. Jesus wept because He saw it differently. While other people wouldn't think twice about the city, He wept. He wept because He saw *into* the city. He saw the families, couples, and kids. He saw the hurting, the broken, the distant, and it so moved Him because His one agenda on planet Earth is to reach people.

Cities are known for a lot of things: famous buildings, sports teams, even certain industries, but Jesus sees the lost, the empty. However, He doesn't just stop there, because He also sees potential. He sees the lost, found, and the hurting, healed. The empty, filled, and the broken, restored. Aren't you grateful He saw us that way?

When was the last time you wept over your city? We don't typically think this way. In the Bay Area in California, there is major traffic. There's also a train that commuters will ride. When driving home in this traffic, people are not naturally given to thinking about all the people around them who are far from God. Usually, it's just the thought of, "Hurry up, get home, eat dinner, and relax."

But what if you changed the way you saw people? What if this week, instead of hurrying to get where you need to go, you pause and ask God to help you see people the way He sees them? What if you gave some of that time in traffic to pray for your city? Even for the people driving right next to you? How would your domino affect people? Who knows the impact we could have? God does.

I once walked our city and the one next to it, from one side to the other. It took me three days, at several hours a day. In the Bible, it records in Joshua 1:3 that "I will give you every place where you set your foot." So I decided to walk the area and ask God to give it to us so we could reach people with His love. Something interesting happened as I walked and prayed. God gave me a picture into the houses in the area. On one side of the city I saw emptiness. On the other side of the city I saw brokenness. I wept as I walked. My heart was broken for the people in the city. It's interesting that God gave us two words for our church a long time ago: Hope and Healing. Hope for tomorrow and Healing from yesterday. But I never made the connection until one day I was describing what God showed me, and in the middle of the sermon, I felt the Lord say, "The two words I gave for the church is a fulfillment for the two words I showed you when you walked your city. For emptiness, I have given hope. For brokenness, I have given healing." I literally had to stop in the middle of the sermon because I had never connected the dots before this moment.

What happened? Walking the city caused me to see it differently. And since then we have seen the domino effect of one life touching another and another. I'm glad we never quit in all the dips we've experienced because we are now seeing one life touching several and several lives touching thousands. Don't you want to reach people with God's love? It starts with one. It starts with you.

Did you know that one of our greatest distractions is ourselves? That selfie syndrome. You can't see the hurting when you're too close to the mirror. When your focus is on yourself, how can you recognize the person standing right in front of you who is in need of what you have to give? When we want what we want instead of wanting what God wants, we begin to step out of our destinies. Jonah was a guy like this.

When we want what we want instead of wanting what God wants, we begin to step out of our destinies.

God called Jonah to go preach to the city of Nineveh. Jonah heard that call and ran in the opposite direction. He literally got on a boat headed the opposite way! He saw Nineveh as an old broken-down house, like Dianna's and my fix-and-flip, but God saw amazing potential. As he was fleeing from God's call, a storm hit, one that terrified everyone on board. He finally told the crew, "It's my fault, guys. I'm in disobedience to God and you're experiencing a storm because of me. If you throw me overboard, the storm will cease." And so they did! They hurled him overboard, and he was swallowed by a great fish, and he remained in its belly for three days. On the third day, Jonah repented and the fish vomited him out. (Side thought: You might be walking through a storm that doesn't even belong to you. Some of your storms are only a result of your proximity to someone else's disobedience. That was for free. You're welcome.)

When he finally arrived in Nineveh, he *walked* the city, which was so large that it took three days for him to go through it (Jonah 3:3). One would think that his heart would have broken for that city that was so corrupt and lost. He finally preached, and the whole city turned to God.

It was an amazing revival! And one would also think that he'd be happy. An entire city turning to God? We would be thrilled. Not Jonah. He climbed on a hill and he was angry. He wanted to see the fireworks display of God's judgment over the city to the tune of Sodom and Gomorrah, but instead God had mercy on every person in the city. Jonah got angry and started pouting to God: "Isn't this what I said, Lord, when I was still at home? That is what I tried to forestall by fleeing to Tarshish. I knew that you are a gracious and compassionate God, slow to anger and abounding in love, a God who relents from sending calamity. Now, Lord, take away my life, for it is better for me to die than to live" (Jonah 4:2–3).

Unbelievable! Jonah's acting like a little brat. He's angry at God for showing kindness to the city and forgiving people there. He's asking God to just take his life. Are you kidding me? Selfie syndrome on steroids. But then God shuts him up by telling him, "Should I not have concern for the great city of Nineveh, in which there are more than a hundred and twenty thousand people who cannot tell their right hand from their left?" (Jonah 4:11).

God says there's a hundred twenty thousand people who don't know their right hand from their left. He could be talking about babies or people who just can't see right from wrong yet. One thing is for sure, God loved that city and didn't just want to write it off, but instead desired to forgive and restore it. So He used Jonah to push the first domino. But the problem wasn't that Jonah didn't see the city; he just didn't see it the way *God* saw it. Jonah saw sin and rebellion. God saw restoration and healing.

I was speaking about this one time and someone came up to me and said, "My wife and I loved the sermon today. Jonah preached to the Ninevites, who are my wife's ancestors, the Assyrians. They became one of the first and few Christians in the Middle East. To this day, some Assyrians still celebrate the day of Jonah and thank God for his impact." God has a plan.

You can see people but not really see them the way God sees them. You can notice them but not really see them. You can observe them and not have a heart for them. God loves the world and He wants us to as well. Let's ask God for a new prescription to see people the way He sees people.

SELFIE SYNDROME TO SERVANT MENTALITY

Joseph was thrown into a pit. A literal dip. But I gotta say, as a young teen, flexing around in his many-colored coat and bragging about his dreams to his brothers wasn't the smartest thing to be doing. He *knew* his relationship with his brothers was not favorable, to say the least, and yet he allowed his selfie syndrome to dig an even deeper wedge—until finally they got rid of him.

Sold into slavery, he worked at Potiphar's house until he was elevated to second in command of the entire house because he served so well. The Scripture tells us that Potiphar gave everything to Joseph and didn't concern himself with anything under Joseph's care. We can see humility starting to do its work in Joseph's heart, and maybe he began seeing everyone around him more like God saw them.

When Potiphar's wife tried to get him to sleep with her, by now Joseph was such a man of integrity that he ran away. She then lied and accused him of rape. Potiphar had him thrown in prison for something he didn't do. Potiphar knew the integrity of Joseph and he knew his wife. That's probably why he only threw Joseph in prison because the penalty for such a crime, in this culture, would have been death. But he had to do something to appease his bride.

Again we see that while in prison, Joseph served so well that the warden elevated him to second in command and didn't concern himself with anything under Joseph's care. Joseph's character had risen to the point where God could now use him to save nations. Joseph no longer was blinded by a selfie syndrome; he now had a servant mentality. He was brought out of prison and elevated to second in command of the entire nation of Egypt, and Pharaoh didn't concern himself with anything under Joseph's care.

Are we that reliable? Proverbs 25:19 says, "Putting confidence in an unreliable person in times of trouble is like chewing with a broken tooth or walking on a lame foot" (NLT). You can't lean on them or put any weight on them. Are we reliable? Can we ask God to help us see as He sees? Can God count on us to be faithful with His mission of reaching people with His love? Are we open to be used to serve others even when we feel like we're in a dip? Let's let Joseph's life inspire ours. He journeyed from a selfie syndrome to a servant mentality. Serving is what literally got him out of the dip. Serving is how he left all his dips behind.

Some people come out of their dip and do nothing, but God does not bring you out of your dip to be dormant. He is calling you to something. Calling you, as 1 Peter 2:9 tells us, "out of darkness into his wonderful light." When God calls you out of the dip of darkness, He also calls you into your deliberate destiny: His purpose of serving others. The goal is not just to come out of the dip; the goal is to understand what He's calling you into.

There have been baseball players who were in a slump. When someone in a slump finally hit a home run, they didn't just stand there and go back to the dugout. No. They ran the bases. Once you give your life to Jesus and come out of your dip, don't just stand there. Don't make the most important decision of your life and do nothing. Run the bases! Get involved in and join a Bible-believing church. Get into a small group of other believers who are going in the same direction as you. Discover your gifts. Use those

God does not bring you out of your dip to be dormant. He is calling you to something.

gifts to make a difference in other people's lives. Be the domino that sets thousands to flight!

God, help us to see people the way You see them. See, care, respond. Ask yourself, "Can I see people as Jesus sees them? Can I serve people as Jesus serves them? Can I see Jesus in them?" Matthew 25:35–40 gives us an example of how God sees people:

> "For I was hungry, and you fed me. I was thirsty, and you gave me a drink. I was a stranger, and you invited me into your home. I was naked, and you gave me clothing. I was sick, and you cared for me. I was in prison, and you visited me."
>
> Then these righteous ones will reply, "Lord, when did we ever see you hungry and feed you? Or thirsty and give you something to drink? Or a stranger and show you hospitality? Or naked and give you clothing? When did we ever see you sick or in prison and visit you?" And the King will say, "I tell you the truth, when you did it to one of the least of these my brothers and sisters, you were doing it to me!" (NLT)

I once heard Joseph Stowell say that God knows how much you love Him by how you treat people. That's the test. I know you're thinking, *Can I have another test?* Because people are not the easiest to love. But this is the test. So, I guess I should say, don't miss Jesus. Don't overlook Jesus. We may have missed opportunities in the past but let's commit to not miss anymore. See people like Jesus sees them. Serve people like Jesus. Because we don't want to miss Jesus. Compassion without action is just sympathy. Sympathy never changed the world. Let God's love move us into action. Push the next domino. Because dominos do not push themselves.

Chapter 21

GET UP FROM THE TABLE

It was Thursday night and getting dark. Everyone in Jerusalem was finding a place to pause, reflect, and celebrate a meal called Passover. (This was an annual Jewish feast to remember the time when God passed over those in Egypt who had the blood of a lamb over their doorpost. If you've seen *The Prince of Egypt*, you're basically caught up to speed.)

Jesus and His twelve disciples also gathered in a rented room to partake in the Last Supper. John 13:1 helps set the scene: "It was just before the Passover Festival. Jesus knew that the hour had come for him to leave this world and go to the Father. Having loved his own who were in the world, he loved them to the end."

Jesus understood His time was coming to an end and that tomorrow He was going to the cross. And yet, with the weight of all this on His mind, He still served. He still *showed them* the full extent of His love. That's a heavy statement. And as we are about to see, the full extent of His love was demonstrated by serving. Love is not just spoken, it's shown. I'm so grateful that Jesus didn't just drive by and tell us He loved us, but I'm over-the-top thankful that He showed us by laying down His life for us to be forgiven and set free.

SAVED TO SERVE

Allow me to paint the picture of this setting. Some men had been planning Jesus' death for a while, and now they were ready to act. The disciples were clueless as to what was about to take place, preoccupied with themselves and jockeying for position. Judas was there, too, just to give you a feel for the room.

The disciples all entered this upper room and immediately started talking and hanging out. Culturally, few people in that era had baths at home. As Ray Stedman points out, the people would go to the Roman baths to clean up for a special occasion like this. But even then, in their New Testament Crocs, and after walking the dirty roads of that day, their feet got filthy by dinnertime. In preparation for a meal like this, normally a house had a servant to wash feet. This was reserved for the lowest guy on the roster. He got stuck with foot duty.

I get why no servant would've wanted that job because—can we all agree?—feet are not the prettiest part of the human body. I was thinking recently, at what point do feet transition? At what point do feet transition from being cute to just being gross? Baby feet are cute. Parents take their baby's feet and play with them, saying things with a baby voice: "Look at the little toe-toes. Look at these little feet. Cute little feet. This little piggy went to market..." They put their baby's feet on their face. They put their baby's feet in their mouth. They bite their toes. You ain't never done that to your grandpa.

True story. My grandpa, when he was ninety, had his two big toenails removed because of ingrown toenail problems. My grandpa asked the doctor if he could take them home. Yes, he did! My grandpa brought his two-inch toenails home in a little pill bottle, called us all into the living room, where he was reclining on his La-Z-Boy, and asked if we wanted to see his toenails. I said, "Grandpa, you could make earrings out of those and give them to Grandma to wear." I can just see Grandma shaking her head with the earrings dangling about. Our family has a twisted sense of humor. "No! Grandpa! We don't want to see your toenails!"

Then he said, "I need someone to rub ointment over the place where they removed the toenails on my big toes." My brother and I walked straight out of the room and left my wife, Dianna, in there by herself. She did it! She's a servant, that one. I couldn't bring myself to do it.

Feet are gross. Have you ever looked down at someone's feet and thought to yourself, "Wow. Those feet have some mileage on them." Have you ever had to take a second look because, for a second there, you thought they had one too many piggies? You even start to count, "Seven, eight, nine…ten. Huh. I guess there are just ten." But the way they were all stacked on top of each other led you to believe there might have been an extra one. Feet looking like a pile of newborn pugs. Like their feet are throwing up gang signs.

Dianna asked me one time if I'd like to get a pedicure with her. I thought that sounded nice. But it wasn't! It was torture! This lady took a steak knife and started jabbing it under my toenail. I'm screaming, "Make it stop! Make it stop!" Then she grabbed this cheese grater–like tool and started shredding fresh parmesan cheese off my heel. She was wearing gloves and a mask. I don't blame her. I would've been wearing a hazmat suit. And I'm convinced she was talking about me the whole time.

All of that to say, "Feet are nasty!" At the Last Supper, no one volunteered to wash feet. All the disciples walked into the room that night, and all of them would have seen the water basin used for foot washing. But they walked right by that basin to get to their seat at the table. They were more concerned with their seat at the table than serving someone else.

Have you ever had a parent say, "Come in this kitchen and clean up this mess!" Then you and any siblings you have all yell back, "It's not my turn!" This is essentially the same thing we do when Jesus asks us to serve others. What you were saying was: "It's not my responsibility." But we will never do what we don't take responsibility for. We say, "Someone else will do it." This helps us feel justified in not doing it because we think someone else will get to it. "I'm too busy." Well, everyone is busy. Jesus was busy but that didn't stop Him from serving.

Luke records that after everyone had settled in at the table, Jesus gave them a picture of communion. Imagine this in your mind. Jesus and His disciples were sitting in a dark room lit by candlelight. They were celebrating Passover, like they had done their entire lives; only this time, Jesus changed the normal script about the Passover lamb used in Egypt and drew them in to point out how He would be the Passover Lamb of God. He began to reveal to them how salvation would now enter human history because He would die and rise again to pay for our sins.

Jesus took some bread, broke it, and said, "This is my body, which is broken for you. This drink is my blood that will be shed for you." Can you sense the emotion in His voice and the urgency in His eyes as He was expressing how He must die for them?

MISSED IT

Check out what happens next: "A dispute also arose among them as to which of them was considered to be greatest. Jesus said to them, '...the greatest among you should be like the youngest, and the one who rules like the one who serves. For who is greater, the one who is at the table or the one who serves? Is it not the one who is at the table? But I am among you as one who serves'" (Luke 22:24–27).

Seriously? Here was Jesus, hours away from going through the most horrific kind of human execution possible. He was pouring His heart out to the twelve closest to Him, and breaking the holy hush in the room, they turn the tables to make it about themselves by asking which of them was the greatest?!

When you're more concerned with your seat at the table, you'll miss what Jesus is trying to teach you.

But Jesus, as full of grace as ever, took the time to answer their ridiculously timed question. He simply taught them that the greatest among them is the one who serves. Have you ever been to a restaurant and had a bad server? All right. Have you ever been to a restaurant and had a good server?

When you're more concerned with your seat at the table, you'll miss what Jesus is trying to teach you.

What makes a good server? A good server goes out of their way for you. Sure, they have other things to do but they go out of their way for you. They're attentive to your needs. They're always asking, "Do you need a refill on your water? Do you need some more bread?" Then they deliver what you need. It's not enough for them to just *see* what you need. It's important for them to actually *deliver* what you need. They bring out the steak and potatoes and the lava cake that oozes chocolate when you cut into the center. And then they clean up your mess. That makes a great server.

Listen. Jesus did (and does) all of these things for us. Jesus went out of His way for us. He came to Earth to give His life so we could be forgiven and be offered eternal life with Him. He is attentive to our needs. He knows what we have need of before we even ask. He delivers to us what we need. He will supply our needs according to His riches in glory. And aren't you glad that He loved us enough to step into time and space to clean up our mess of sin? Jesus served us in the best possible way.

Jesus was about to blow their minds at this Last Supper. "So [Jesus] got up from the table…" (John 13:4 NLT). The very table that all the disciples made sure they had a good seat at. The very table they came to be fed at. The very table they all came to, while walking past a water basin and the opportunity to serve because they were expecting someone else to serve them.

Instead of going out of their way, they sat at the table. Instead of being attentive to someone else's needs, they sat at the table. Instead of giving others what they needed, they sat at the table. Instead of helping clean up their mess, they sat at the table. If we're not careful, we can fall into the same self-centered approach to life.

Jesus saw this and decided to set an example by getting up from the table. The disciples were all watching, waiting, wondering what He was doing, but they were not prepared for what He did next. If anyone deserved to be served, it was Jesus. And to give them a picture they would never forget, Jesus slowly got up from the table, walked over to the water basin, and filled it. He took off His outer garments, grabbed a towel, and then got down on His hands and knees. Here was the King of kings, and the Lord of lords, the Maker of heaven and earth, and He stooped down and washed the feet of everyone in the room. Including Judas, who would betray Him!

They didn't know how to act. Peter tried to stop Him. Others sat in silence and disbelief. They knew they all should've done this for Him, but now He was doing this for them.

After He was finished washing all of their feet, He "returned to his place at the table" (John 13:12 GNT). See, Jesus had a place at the table. But He was willing to give up His place to serve others.

Jesus then asked, "Do you understand what I have done for you?… Now that I, your Lord and Teacher, have washed your feet, you also should wash one another's feet. I have set you an example that you should do as I have done for you" (John 13:12, 14–15). This wasn't about foot washing. Sometimes we can see the illustration but miss the message. Washing feet isn't even a part of our culture today. He wasn't saying to start the First Church of the Foot Washing. He told them, "I've left you an *example* to follow." In other words: serve people.

It's interesting that when they asked Jesus who was the greatest, He never told them that was a bad question. He didn't say desiring to be great was wrong. He just clearly defined what greatness looked like. We might think greatness is a large social media platform or a huge influence. Jesus pointed to the beauty of a muddy towel and declared that this is greatness.

Jesus said, "Now that I've shown you, I want you to do this for others." Jesus was the greatest undercover boss in the world. He didn't just bark orders; He demonstrated how He wanted to be presented through us.

So many of us want influence and leadership. I've heard it said, "If serving is beneath you, then leadership is beyond you."

Listen, I know it's comfortable at the table, but there comes a time when we've got to get up from the table. I know it's a good place to start; that's why we've set the table for people to begin with. But at some point, we've got to get up from the table. I know it feels nice to have other people serve you, but at some point, we've got to get up from the table.

How long will we sit at the table? How long will we make it all about us? Tell yourself, I'm getting up from the table. Jesus was giving us a clue. We think that we'll get full by just sitting at the table, but fulfillment comes by getting up from the table and serving others for Jesus' sake.

Proverbs 11:25 teaches us, "Those who refresh others will themselves be refreshed." We think it's like young kids in line for the water fountain, where one kid is so thirsty that he's fighting to get to the front to get a drink to refresh himself. That's how we approach life a lot of the time. We think to ourselves, *I'm thirsty! I've got to focus on me. I've got to get to the front of the line so I can get a drink.* But Proverbs tells us God works differently. God says, if you refresh others, I will personally guarantee your own refreshment.

When I have felt seasons of depression try to creep in, my natural tendency was to stay home, close the blinds, and focus on me. But I found that depression broke off when I made up my mind to serve someone every day. I came alive when I got out of the selfie-syndrome dip and chose to prefer others.

Maybe it's time for you to get up from the table and get involved in serving at a church. Or for some of you, maybe it's time to lead a small group for other people to be able to come to Jesus. What about signing up to serve in some capacity with your city or to go on a mission trip? See people the way Jesus sees them and find a way to serve them in your city. Jesus served us and was giving us a pattern. He said, "What I have done for you, I want you to do for others." Serve others. Add value, period. When you do, you'll earn the right to share your faith. I believe the next wave of revival to sweep the world will not be through another conference or worship song. It's going to come when the average Christian wins their sphere to Jesus by serving and adding value to those people's lives.

THE PATTERN

When I was young, I loved to draw. I started by getting books that I could trace. I'd get some tracing paper, lay it over the pattern, and simply copy the pattern. People who saw my art thought I was a talented artist, but really, I was just a good tracer. Jesus has laid out His life as a pattern. Let's lay our lives over His and just trace the way He loves people. Trace the way He serves people. Trace the way He goes out of His way for others. Let's trace how He's attentive to the needs of others and how He delivers what they need and, with joy, cleans up the mess of others.

God knows how much you love Him by how you treat people.

God knows how much you love Him by how you treat people. One time, a religious leader asked Jesus which was the greatest commandment. Jesus responded by instructing him to love the Lord your God with all your heart, soul, mind, and strength (see Mark 12:28–34). The guy only asked for one, but Jesus knew you cannot divorce the first commandment from the second, so He added that you should love your neighbor as yourself.

Remember, we are to serve people as if they *are* Jesus. Picture His face over their shoulders and allow God's love in us to move us to action. Love is not love until it moves us to *do* something. "Let's not merely say that we love each other; let us show the truth by our actions" (1 John 3:18 NLT). Love without action is just sympathy.

How many water basins have we walked by? How many opportunities have we walked by because we wanted a seat at the table? But God has given us all a towel. It represents our time, talents, and resources. And for most of us, we have been trying to keep our towel clean and pristine. But when we get to heaven, God's not going to be excited that our towel is clean: He wants us to see the beauty of a muddy towel.

Jesus needed to make sure His disciples truly understood this, so He gave them a picture they would never forget, and said, "Remember Me! Remember this towel. Remember this moment. Remember this example. Get up from the table and serve others in My name and you will become great in the kingdom of God!"

It could be that today you feel like your feet are dirty, symbolically. Interestingly enough, feet represent where we go and where we've been. Jesus wants to wash you clean, no matter your shortcomings or failures. Jesus washed Judas' feet, fully aware Judas was going to betray Him in just a few hours. This means that Jesus knows what you're going to do and still wants to wash you clean. Maybe you've been sitting at the table for too long and you're feeling like it's time to push back from the table and begin to serve others like Jesus.

It's funny. Sometimes we'll go to a restaurant and they tell us there's a wait. We'll wait for fifteen minutes. Thirty minutes. We have waited for an hour before to get into a restaurant. They give us that little buzzer. Our friends ask us to walk around and we say, "No. I don't want to be out of range when our buzzer goes off."

So we sit there and we wait. And we wait. What are we waiting for? We are waiting for someone who is already at a table to get up from the table and to make room for us to have a place at the table. It's frustrating when people who have eaten at the table are finished but they refuse to get up from the table, even though they see a line of people outside, waiting.

I'm praying that through this book, we get God's heart to come to the table, and to let Jesus cleanse us and pour into us. But then I'm praying that we won't just be focused on us but that we will turn around and notice the hundreds of thousands of hungry people waiting to get in. That we will be willing to say, "Do you need a seat? Here, take my seat. I'm willing to get up for you. Can I get you anything? Can I serve you? Can I encourage you? Can I pray for you? I'm willing to get up from my seat at the table so you can have a place here too."

Even at church. Church becomes really fun when you stop coming just for you. And you'll never even know what purpose feels like until you're making a difference in someone else's life. Maybe it's time to give up your seat that you *always* sit in and offer it to someone else. Better yet, become part of the team so you can serve them with the gifts God's given you to make a difference for eternity.

No one has ever lived only for themselves and fulfilled God's purpose for their life. Let's personally welcome people and escort them to their seats at the table, where their life, too, will be forever changed by the love of Jesus.

You don't have to stay stuck. As a matter of fact, you're not stuck; you just stopped moving. Let's get up from the table. Pick up your towel and wash the feet of the cities God's called us to. There are others God wants you to reach on the other side of your dip. So let's go make some more stories together. Start right now, by encouraging someone to keep going by texting them, "Don't quit in the dip."

Afterword

IF YOU'RE NOT DEAD, GOD'S NOT DONE

Many people work the graveyard shift. It's a middle-of-the-night shift that can be brutal. There's an old folktale that claims the history behind the name of these midnight work hours. During the 1800s in England, the death tolls caused by lead poisoning and other diseases were climbing at such a high rate there was a graveyard plot shortage! Some less reputable cemetery owners began to exhume countless coffins in order to reuse the plots for other corpses. To their shock, one in twenty-five coffins contained scratch marks and shredded interiors. They deduced that, due to lead poisoning, these poor souls had fallen into a comatose state only to be buried alive. One remedy was to tie a string around the wrist of everyone who they buried and for that string to go up to the ground level and be tied to a bell. The person hired to keep watch all night over those bells sat through the *graveyard shift*. At the first tinkling of a bell, that man was to grab his shovel and dig like mad to rescue the person buried alive. SCARIEST. JOB. EVER.

Whether this old legend is true or not, it serves as a great analogy. You may relate to feeling buried alive by stress, or circumstances, or even wrong choices. Buried under the heaviness of doubt, insecurities, and fear. You might feel like you have been trying to scratch and claw your way out on your own, but to no avail.

I'm so glad we have a God who works the graveyard shift! He never sleeps or breaks His watch, and He's been waiting for you to ring the bell of faith. At the first tinkling of that prayer, He comes running to rescue you and dig you out of your dip. Alone, we are left hopeless in the pit of our despair. But Jesus is "the resurrection and the life" (John 11:25).

Let me say this again: God wants to rescue you out of your dip! He doesn't want you to stay in a place of discouragement or failure. No matter how you got there, He wants to bring you out. I know it may not look good now, but don't quit in the dip. Taking a look across the landscape of modern history, athletics, and entertainment, we can find many examples of people who earned the admiration of our generation. Whether reaching a level of success in business or sports or family, some of these people would have been long forgotten had they quit in the dip.

God wants to rescue you out of your dip! He doesn't want you to stay in a place of discouragement or failure.

Michael Jordan was cut from his high school basketball team.

In 1922, Walt Disney, due to his company not making ends meet, was living out of his office and taking baths once a week at Union Station.

Oprah Winfrey was dropped from her first job as co-anchor for the evening news at a Baltimore ABC affiliate.

Henry Ford left his comfortable job to establish the Detroit Automobile Company. In just over a year, it went bankrupt. He rallied investors in 1901 but went bankrupt again. He tried a third time in 1903 and became a huge success when he released the Model T.

The Formula 409 cleaner got its name from two young scientists determined to make the ultimate grease-cutting cleaner on the market. They didn't get the chemical recipe right until the 409th try.

History is replete with story after story of people who had every reason to quit in the dip but didn't. And they went on to accomplish incredible things. I wonder how many more heroes we could've heard about throughout history, but we never got the privilege to know them or their contribution on the earth because they quit.

Another real-world example of someone who didn't quit in the dip was a man by the name of Winston Churchill. I had the honor of receiving an invite from John C. Maxwell to have a private tour through Winston Churchill's bunker in London, along with Winston Churchill's grandson. We were able to go into the war room, even venture behind the Plexiglas, to see Churchill's chair, the arm of which he had worn down with his ring. We saw his briefcase. His cigar. His map. It was surreal.

Churchill was the one who led England through the toughest of times and defeated Nazi Germany. And he did it all while he was well advanced in years. He stayed the course and saved the world. It wasn't in his twenties. It wasn't in his thirties or forties. He was seventy-one years old when he helped save the day.

He received poor grades in almost every subject except history and English composition. He almost didn't make it into military school, as he failed the first two attempts. He had a lisp, which he had a hard time correcting. But he didn't quit at school. He eventually was elected to Parliament and formulated a massive attack in World War I that epically failed. But he didn't quit. He was even voted out of office before World War II. Had he died in 1939, he would've died a failure. No one listened to him until 1940.

He was famous for saying, "There are no victories in retreat and defeat." As I stood in his war room, I saw something that I will never forget. It was a sign he had placed on the table, across from where many of the greatest military minds gathered to discuss the war and strategize. Three of these leaders constantly told Churchill what couldn't be done, so he placed in clear view of them these words, written by Queen Victoria during the Boer War:

> Please understand there is no depression in this house and we are not interested in the possibilities of defeat. They do not exist.

Whenever there was a bombing in London, he would go directly to the site of the bombing for a picture. Just to let the world know that they were still standing.

Winston Churchill was an unapologetic, stalwart hero who never quit. Think about it. Where would Nazi Germany be today? Where would England be? And America? And the world? What would the destruction have been had he left his post? But he didn't quit. He led the world out of World War II and became the hero of England.

My favorite quote that's frequently attributed to him is, "Success is going from failure to failure without losing your enthusiasm." I want to be him when I grow up. No, I want to be him today. Right now. Right here. And so can you. You can be the Winston Churchill to your family. Your school. Your workplace. Your generation. You are the Joseph. The Peter. The Esther. The Mary. The David. The Paul. Never give up. Use the truths inside this book to embolden you and to remind you who you really are: a child of God filled with the power of the Holy Spirit.

Jesus promised that we would do greater things than He did. But you have to come out of the dip to make a difference in your world. No matter if you feel buried alive, there is still breath in your lungs, so ring that bell of faith and allow God to refresh and revive your soul. There is still destiny to accomplish. Lessons to be learned. People to help and inspire. And a world to reach.

If you're not dead, God's not done.

DON'T QUIT IN THE DIP.

ACKNOWLEDGMENTS

I am extremely grateful for the people who have crossed my path. I am a firm believer that God allows divine intersections along life's journey. Some for you to help and some to receive help from. What may have seemed like an accident or a fluke moment turned into a significant piece of a relational puzzle to accomplish God's purposes.

I will forever be indebted to my wife, Dianna. You have loved me more than I deserve and have held on to God's promises in times when my faith was wavering. You are a significant part of the reason I didn't quit in the dip.

To our four girls, I want to say that raising you has been the greatest joy of my life. I'm so thankful that God allowed Mom and me to be your parents. I love you so much.

Thank you to my dad and mom, for instilling faith in me at a young age to believe in the power of prayer and to trust in God.

An enormous thank-you to Chris Hodges. When I was at my lowest point, God used you to display clear steps of faith and strategy that brought my soul back to life. The word *mentor* seems to fall short of accurately describing your heart and influence. You are truly a spiritual father to this generation and I'm better because of you.

Thank you to Dr. John Maxwell for taking me under your wing. You continue to stretch my thinking and capacity as a leader. You add value to people like no one I've ever seen. I am beyond blessed to have you in my life.

Rick Bezet, you have been such a blessing to my life. I have never had a conversation with you where I didn't leave encouraged. You are the best at loving people.

Thank you to editor Molly Venzke. How you prayerfully approached this project pointed me in the right direction and helped to establish my thought process with greater clarity.

Thank you to Worthy Publishing for partnering with me. It was an honor to work with you.

I am so thankful for the staff and the congregation of Fellowship Church. Your heart to sacrifice and serve others never ceases to amaze me. I am tremendously humbled and amazed that God would allow me to be your pastor.

And I've saved the most important for last: Jesus. I weep as I write this, for You have been with me every step of the way. You've never left me alone, and I now know that You allowed me to go through my dip to help others know it can be done through You. You truly are the Way, the Truth, and the Life. It is my extreme honor and great privilege to serve You.

ABOUT THE AUTHOR

SHAUN NEPSTAD has a passion to help people who feel stuck. Through speaking, writing, and helping people build teams, his desire is that everyone would not only discover but also walk in their full potential. He is a sought-after leader, communicating around the world with business and church people alike. Shaun, along with his wife, Dianna, founded Fellowship Church in Antioch, California, in 2002. Under their leadership the church has grown to over five thousand in weekly attendance. He has spoken all over the globe and carries with him the message of hope and healing. Shaun has a desire to train leaders and a unique ability to teach about how to build and strengthen teams. He and Dianna have four daughters. You can follow him on social media @shaunnepstad.